# Life in the Gardeners' Bothy

**Dad and his chrysanthemums at Bemerton Court in 1927.**

# Life in the Gardeners' Bothy

Arthur Hooper

MALTHOUSE PRESS
2000

First published by Malthouse Press, Suffolk, 2000.



ISBN 0 9522355 9 5

**British Library Cataloguing-in-Publication Data**

A catalogue record for this book is
available from the British Library.



Designed by Robert Malster.
Typeset by John Walton.
Printed in Great Britain by
Wolsey Press, Ipswich.

# Contents


Foreword vi

1 Head Gardeners' son 1

2 The Bothy boys 9

3 On the wheel 19

4 Alarms and excursions 26

5 Friends and poachers 36

6 Work and play 42

7 A hard winter 54

8 Celebrations 64

9 An unpleasant change 71

10 The Chelsea Flower Show 83

11 An unexpected visit 90

12 Summary promotion 99

13 Heavy duty and cricket 111

14 Exotic plants 125

15 General foreman 138

16 Horses and washing up 146

17 The party season 157

18 Leaving the bothy 166

19 Head Gardener at last 174


To my dear wife,
Dorothy

# Foreword

Arthur Hooper is a member of probably the last generation to experience life in the gardeners' bothy, the simple and sometimes primitive building in a corner of the garden of stately homes that housed the unmarried men who worked in the garden.

Born into an England that was ruled over by King Edward VII and was the centre of a great empire, he grew up in an age of certainties. Everyone paid due respect to the Squire and his Lady, and as a boy he learnt also to respect his parents, who were always there to see that he grew up in what they and thousands of others regarded as "the right way". His father was a Head Gardener, a man who wielded authority within his own garden, for all that it was owned by the man who employed him.

Young Arthur never wanted to do anything other than work in the garden and, eventually, to become a Head Gardener like his father. Throughout this book the title Head Gardener is written with capital letters. Modern English usage would have it otherwise, but to Arthur's generation a Head was a man to whom respect had to be given; he had earned his position through years of hard work and hard learning, and his title deserved those capital letters, whatever anyone might think of his treatment of his men or his attitudes.

Some bothies might be little better than hovels, but the bothy was more than a place in which to live, it was a tiny community with its own strict rules which could never be broken. Arthur's story is of a community that was, and is, little known to outsiders.

It was unfortunate that when he at last achieved his aim of becoming a Head Gardener the outbreak of the Second World War robbed him of his job. In a world of certainties he expected to be called up for the Forces, but certainties were becoming something from another age. Instead it was decreed that, as he had gone back to working with his father, and his father was producing food in the gardens of a Wiltshire mental hospital, he was doing work of national importance and would not be called up.

Everything had changed when he resumed his search for a Head's job after the war. Whereas in the Twenties and Thirties a large garden had employed twenty or thirty men, he had only four men under him in his first post-war position. Everything else might have changed, but the soil was the same, the plants were the same, and the old skills were still required.

Today, with his ninetieth birthday behind him, Arthur finds his gardening skills are still in demand. It might be on television or it might be at a brainstorming session at a meeting of some horticultural society in Sussex, not too far from the Gardeners' Royal Benevolent Society home where he now lives in retirement, but whatever the place Arthur speaks with authority – the authority of a Head Gardener.

Robert Malster

Holbrook,
*September 2000*

**Arthur Hooper, out in the garden at the age of 91.**

# Head Gardener's son 1

WHEN the school year was divided into terms it was no longer possible to leave school on one's fourteenth birthday, as one had done up to then. As I was fourteen in October I could not start work until the New Year of 1922, when I joined my father in the gardens of Bemerton Lodge, Salisbury.

I had always wanted to work in the garden, and my father did nothing to dissuade me; it seemed so natural for me to follow him as he had made a success of gardening himself. He was Head Gardener to Sir Cecil Chubb, who at that time employed seventeen men and boys in his gardens. Sir Cecil was the man who gave Stonehenge to the nation. Being Head, my father had under him a foreman in the glasshouses with three men and two boys; in the pleasure grounds there was a foreman in charge of four men and a boy; and in the kitchen garden there was a foreman with four men and two boys. The garden carter was an elderly man who did odd jobs around the mansion as well as being in charge of the garden horse.

This was a normal set-up in the country estate garden. By the standing ruling at that time, our garden was of no great importance; it was rather small, although it did rate a mention in *The Gardener's Chronicle* list of good-class gardens.

All my life I had lived on this estate, and I had grown used to the pattern of living where the Squire and his Lady were the all-important persons, to whom everyone paid due respect. I had been taught that whenever I saw Sir Cecil or Lady Chubb out walking I was to keep out of sight if at all possible, but if they passed by in their carriage I must acknowledge them by a touch of my cap.

I started work as a boy in the glasshouses, where I did the usual boy's work of pot-washing, soil-sieving, greenhouse-washing and general chores, at the same time learning how to handle plants and later even being allowed to do some potting and watering. After a year I was moved into the kitchen garden, also for a year, digging, hoeing and even planting. My next twelve months were spent learning pleasure ground work, then I was brought back into the glasshouses as an improver. All this gave me basic training in the more important departments in the gardens of stately homes.

My father worked me very hard, and I was doing many hours of my own time without thought of payment; he often said that if I was going to be a gardener then I must make sure to master my profession. The training he gave me was tough, but even then I knew it would serve me in good stead later in my life. I enjoyed working with nature and realised quite early that gardening was what I wanted to do; I felt it was the one job in which I would be happy.

When I was almost eighteen my father decided it was time I left home and went into a larger garden to gain further experience. I had known for some time that this day had to come, for my father had often told me that my training would really start on the day I left home to make my own way in the world. It was then that I went into a bothy for the first time.

The bothy to which I refer was not a turf-walled shieling on a Scottish moor but was, as the *New English Dictionary* of 1932 puts it, "a rough kind of cottage, a hut, a hovel, a place where unmarried labourers are lodged". In this case it was a place where unmarried gardeners were accommodated.

I was sent to work for a Mr. H. Mills, who was Head Gardener to Mr. H. Morrison, M.P., and Lady Mary Morrison at Fonthill House, Tisbury, in Wiltshire, about twelve miles west of Salisbury. When I went by the Southern Railway train that day in October, 1925, to Tisbury it was my first experience of a train journey on my own. In fact the only other time I remember being on a train was when, several years before, I had had a short but very rough and dirty ride on the footplate of an engine with a school friend whose father was an engine driver.

It was now up to me to make sure I got out at the right station, I thought as I waited on the platform, nobody was going to help me from now on. It was all up to me, I told myself as the train came puffing into the station in a cloud of steam and smoke. It stopped with a squeal of brakes, a score or so people got out, and others got in, a porter on the platform shouting out the names of the stations at which the train would stop. I made for one of the compartments near the guard's van; I have never been quite sure why I did this, perhaps because I wanted to see the guard wave his flag, or was it because there was an elderly lady sitting in that compartment and I thought I needed her company? I attempted conversation by passing the time of day, but she ignored my presence, which rather hurt.

Within a minute or so I heard a whistle, saw the guard wave his green flag, and with a snort from the engine, a loud puff and a cloud of smoke we moved away from the platform. The puffing got faster and faster as the train gathered speed, and it became necessary for me to get up and close the window to keep the smoke and soot from the engine from coming into the compartment. I pulled on the leather strap that lifted the door window into a closed position; it had holes in it so that it was possible to leave the window in one of five partly-open positions by pressing the strap on to a stud fixed to the inside of the door.

As the train gathered speed I so badly wanted to see the countryside from my window seat, but at times the view was completely blotted out by the smoke. All I could do was turn my attention to what was in our compartment. The two luggage racks above the seats were supported by shining brass brackets, between which were three pictures of places served by the old London & South Western Railway. The seats, horsehair cushions on wooden benches, with just a wooden bulkhead against which to lean, soon began to feel very hard. I was travelling third class as this cost less than second class, and very much less than first class, which could boast of sprung seats and armrests.

It was not long before we stopped at the next station, where my lady companion alighted, still without saying a word. Her place was taken by a man, his wife and two children who had brought with them a picnic hamper, so the children were soon pestering their parents for something to eat. It seemed they had a long journey ahead of them, so they spread out a meal on the opposite seat and the children were soon eating jam sandwiches and drinking mugs of milk. The lady asked me if I would care for some refreshments, and I was pleased to share a cup of tea with them, but I could not settle down as I was so concerned with taking note of the stations at which we stopped. I was somewhat relieved to alight at the right station, where I surrendered my ticket to a porter and was met by the garden carter. Mr. Mills knew the time of my arrival and had sent the garden van to meet the train.

The carter has charge of the garden horse, and it is he who has to do all the carting of goods to and from the garden or to the mansion. He has to cart everything, from coal in a two-wheeled cart to flowers or people in a van, and at times he will be called on to help in the garden, perhaps using a plough in the kitchen garden.

Putting my case in the back, we set off for Fonthill House gardens in the van, drawn by Peter the garden horse, a big dark chesnut, obviously very strong but able to trot briskly along. I relaxed a little, because riding behind a horse, while not as exciting as riding in a train, was much more to my liking. The rattle of the iron-shod wheels on the road was reassuring, and I was able to appreciate the beauty of the countryside in which the trees were taking on their autumn colours. I could note the landmarks at a pace I was more used to, and the peculiar smell of horse and harness always gave me considerable pleasure. I also found pleasure in the power and graceful elegance of the fine animal just before us.

The carter, Jim, was very talkative, and by the time we arrived at the bothy half an hour later I had begun to realise that although bothy life might be fun, work in the gardens was going to be hard and the hours long. Much as I wanted to hear Jim talking about Fonthill, there were times when I was not really listening but was wondering what lay before me, and whether I could make a success of this new venture. I was not feeling too certain of myself, but I had comfort in the thought my mother had left with me when she bade me goodbye, saying "There's always a home for you to return to."

When I first saw it the bothy looked very stark, with its plain stone walls pierced by three windows and a door on the ground floor and three windows above. It had been part of an old mansion that had been demolished years before.

It was about half past four in the afternoon when we arrived at the bothy door. There I was met by the bothy foreman, Bert, who was also foreman in the glasshouses. Knowing that I was a new boy

**The living room of the bothy at Fonthill House, sketched by Toni Goffe.**

to bothy life, Bert lost no time in making me understand that he was in charge of me during and outside working hours, that I would do well to listen to all he had to say and to carry out his instructions to the letter. Having thus been welcomed to the bothy, I was then shown my bedroom, in which were two beds and two rather old wardrobes. One of these, I was told, would be for my use, as were two drawers of a four-drawer chest; those were mine, and only those.

Leaving the case on my bed, we went downstairs to the living room, a large room with a table in the centre and five chairs around it. Against one wall there stood a dresser on which were cups, saucers, plates and various dishes, with three drawers for knives, forks, spoons and cooking utensils.

A black cooking range took up almost all of one end of the

room, while at the other end there was nothing but a row of clothes hooks, most of which were in use. Along the fourth wall, across from the dresser, was a sink with two long wooden draining boards, and with cupboards above and below. The wooden floor was bare except for a mat at the door and another in front of the kitchen range.

A door near the range led to what was known as the sitting room. I had half expected to see some easy chairs, but this was not to be; just two wooden chairs. An open fireplace backed on to the kitchen range. I say an open fireplace, but this was simply a hearth with a few bricks on it to form a fireplace, the modern draught inlet near the hearth being in fact nothing more than a mouse hole in the floorboards.

The only touch of class in the room was a metal fender with a brass rail on its three sides, with two brass seats at the corners. The fire irons, too, had brass handles, and all this metal was kept well polished. On one wall hung a much-used dartboard and a ring board. Together with a shove-ha'penny board on the table, that made up the sum total of the contents of this supposed sitting room.

In each of the two rooms there was an oil lamp hanging from the centre of the ceiling, this being augmented in the living room by a wall lamp with a piece of mirror behind the lamp chimney to act as a reflector. The whole place looked drab and very much in need of a coat of paint, but at least it was clean and reasonably tidy.

Having seen no sign of a toilet, I asked Bert where I would find it. Indeed, it was very much a case of finding it, because Bert directed me outside to the right, then to the right again and, on the forward left, I discovered a wooden shed standing alone and surrounded by trees. I pushed open the door, and there was a seat supported by two heavy beams over a large, deep hole in the ground. The seat was spotlessly clean, the wooden front and top freshly painted, and nearby was a bucket of lime, apparently to be sprinkled into the pit after use with the hand-shovel provided, so keeping the air inside the toilet quite fresh and preventing a hazard from flies. Some newspapers hanging from a nail probably made good reading, but that was not the reason they had been hung there.

A large notice on the inside of the door, clearly to be seen by anyone sitting on the seat, reminded everyone to keep the place clean.

I went back into the bothy to take stock of my surroundings. It was all so very different from what I had been used to at home, yet not unlike what my father had told me to expect. It was adequate, and I felt I could adjust to this new situation. I unpacked most of my case, using the two drawers allocated to me and my one wardrobe, and pondered for a while before going back down the bare wooden stairway to receive a lecture from Bert on bothy law.

It seemed that the worst possible crime was to invite any girlfriends to cross the threshold; commission of this cardinal sin would invite dismissal. No person from outside was allowed to come in if any member of the bothy objected to that person's company. There being five of us living together everything, except our personal belongings, was to be shared between us.

The food was bought by the bothy foreman and the cost shared between us. This was known as the "grub score," and it was up to all of us to keep the score as low as possible, I was told. This statement made me wonder if the standard of living was going to be low, but I felt it was wise at this early stage to keep my counsel and await the turn of events.

Each of us in turn had to do a week of "bothy duty." This meant doing the washing up in the evening, getting in the coal and wood, lighting the fires and keeping them going, taking out the ashes, trimming the wicks of the three oil lamps, making sure there was oil in them, keeping the glass lamp chimneys clean, and generally keeping the place clean and tidy.

The week of "bothy duty" would, I was told, coincide with "garden duty" when the man on duty would have charge of the boilers and all of the glasshouses at weekends and in the evenings. He could be called upon at any time, day or night, to do anything that needed doing. This, in effect, meant that he could not leave the bothy from Friday at five o'clock in the evening, when he started his week of duty, until the next Friday teatime. This was known as being "on the wheel," which was no doubt a reference to the treadwheel that was so much a part of prison life many years ago.

Bert's lecture went on. We had to keep our own bedrooms tidy and, at the weekends, we had to make our own beds and prepare our own food. Why at weekends? I asked. Bert informed me that a woman was employed by the Head Gardener to come into the bothy from Monday to Friday to prepare our breakfast and midday meal, do most of the cleaning, see that our beds were changed each week and to see that the bedding and other household linen was laundered. This was all she was supposed to do, the rest of the work being left to the duty man.

It so happened that our "Mum," as our bothy lady was called, was a widow and did far more for "her boys" than she need have done. She lived nearby, and we were able to help her in many ways, seeing to it that she always had a supply of garden produce in her larder, for instance. This was not difficult to arrange, as the bothy was supplied with vegetables and some fruit as a right, and we were also given our coal and oil as part of our wages, so "Mum" was more than happy with the arrangements we were able to make with her.

With my wages at twenty-four shillings a week, I was told, I should always be able to have some money in my pocket, as our "grub score" never came to more than seven shillings a week. We could be said to be better off than most of the village lads, Bert said, and because we were better off we must always try to keep up appearances, remembering always that we were to be the Head Gardeners of the future.

That, of course, had always been my aim. I was already looking forward to the time when I could earn five pounds a week and have a staff of twenty men or more working under me. I am assured that everyone in bothies had one aim in life, to make the grade as a Head Gardener in one of the many hundreds of good establishments around the country.

# The Bothy boys 2

SOON after half-past five on that first day, Bill, Arthur and Doug came in. These men, with Bert and I, were now the Fonthill House bothy boys. Bert, being foreman, introduced me to the others.

Bill, the foreman in the pleasure gardens, was an Irishman, about thirty, I thought, and he spoke in a broad native dialect that I found difficult to understand. He was friendly enough, but I soon got the impression that I was a mere boy to him and as such I should know my place, treating him as my superior—which, of course, he was.

Arthur was about twenty, a journeyman under Bill, and spoke in a west country dialect that was delightful to listen to; he came from Somerset. Being a journeyman he was on my own level, so I had considerable hopes that he and I might become real pals, as indeed was the case. Doug was the youngest, just seventeen and second journeyman in the plant and fruit houses, so he was my junior both in age and position.

All journeymen were young trainees, and the one whom the Head Gardener considered able to take some responsibility would be first journeyman, directly under the foreman. The younger or less experienced men would be second, third or fourth according to the number of staff under a foreman. I found the position one held in the hierarchy was of considerable importance, so I could consider myself fortunate to have been engaged as first journeyman. I was already gaining benefit from the training my father had given me, and I resolved that when I wrote home I would thank him for all the hard work he had done for me during my early years.

The Head Gardener is supreme, and is therefore to be addressed as "Sir;" his word is law, and nobody would ever dare to question his decisions. He saw to it that we did our work properly, and his orders were carried out to the letter. We were completely in his charge at work, in the bothy and in our spare time. This had to be so if he were to train us up to a standard befitting a Head Gardener.

The Head Gardener's job was very important, not only in terms of the hierarchy on the estate. He had to ensure that anything and everything required in the mansion was available, and that the garden was kept as immaculate as was possible. In order to do this he was careful to employ highly trained foremen whom he could trust to carry out his orders and to ensure that all the men did their work to a high standard.

This being so, the foremen he had engaged assumed a great deal of influence. It was not for them to hire or fire, but should anyone step out of line or fail to do as he was told a word from the foreman to the Head could mean trouble for the person concerned. The foremen had to protect their own jobs, so they were unlikely to allow anything to go wrong in their departments.

One thing I did find was that most Head Gardeners were fair, if firm. If anyone was in difficulty he would usually be summoned to the Head's office, where he would be allowed to explain his point. He would almost certainly receive a lecture, or even a warning, and he might have to apologise for any misdemeanour. We found the best policy was usually to apologise, as of course the foremen were always right, and it was better to be "told off" and keep one's job than to risk dismissal. Work was not easy to find, and without a job one had no income.

It was nearly dark when the five of us sat down to tea. Arthur had already lit the lamps and made good the fire. Bert sat at one end of the table, Bill at the other; Arthur and Doug occupied one side and I had to sit opposite them. This was to be the order of seating at the table, each man in his proper place. The meal was normal fare for working men: bread, butter and jam, with some cake.

Having seen the food laid out on the table my fears of a low standard of living began to evaporate. I was also pleased to see that the meal was properly laid on a tablecloth by Arthur, who was the duty man that week.

The talk at first was about me. They wanted to know where I had come from, and the kind of garden I had been working in. I wondered what their reactions would be when I told them that my father was a Head Gardener, but they did not seem unduly surprised at that and it seemed to matter little to anyone. Having satisfied their curiosity about my background, the conversation turned to gardening. Bert asked me a lot of questions; he wanted to find out what I knew about the subject, what I had been doing and what I really knew about greenhouse plants in particular. I suppose this was quite natural, as I was to be working directly under him, and for the most part under glass.

All this time I had been a little hesitant about taking food. Bill must have noticed this, because he told me I must look after myself or I would go without, as nobody was going to hand me anything to eat. By the time the meal was over I had begun to feel that I was being accepted by my new colleagues, and the tensions which had built up in me gradually relaxed. As I was to live and work with these men it was very important to me that we should at least be friendly towards each other, and already I was beginning to feel that this might not be too difficult after all.

Arthur cleared the table and washed up. It was noticeable that nobody offered to help him, so I asked if I should dry the dishes. Bert immediately told me to leave things well alone, and from the tone of his voice this sounded like an order. Then Arthur got in some coal and kindling wood for the morning, and put out candles ready for anyone who wanted to go up the stairs to the bedrooms. We each had our own candle, which it was necessary to light before going up to our rooms, since there was no lamp on the stairway or in any of the rooms above. After he had lit the fire in the smaller room and taken in some more coal, it appeared to me that Arthur had finished his bothy chores for that day.

During this time the other lads had a wash and clean up, using hot water from the two iron kettles that were kept full and put back on to the kitchen range after use, there to keep company with "Mum's" stock-pot, which was always left on the hotplate to simmer away all the time with any vegetables, meat, bones or anything else "Mum" decided was worth cooking. Arthur and Doug settled down in the sitting room to a game of cribbage, and it was then that I saw a fair collection of books in one corner of the room, mainly gardening books, a few novels and a pile of *The Gardener's Chronicle*.

Bert and Bill, who had changed from their working clothes, said they were going out and asked me if I was going along with them. They did not say where they were going, but it seemed to me that I was expected to go, so the three of us set off together. We walked for about half a mile along a drive which was at first very dark, but as my eyes became accustomed to the gloom I could see fields on either side with cattle still grazing, or taking shelter under large trees that were growing in the parkland. We passed through some lodge gates, where the lodge-keeper came out from his house to see who was opening these large wooden six-bar gates.

When we came to the village there were lights in most of the houses, and the glow of the oil lamps through the curtained windows gave a great feeling of peace and tranquillity. We could see the stark outline of the village church across the road from the King's Head.

It was the King's Head for which we made. We went into the only bar, a large room with a bar counter behind the door as we entered. Behind the bar stood six barrels, all tapped and marked with crosses to denote the strength of the beer inside. In front of the bar the floor was covered with sawdust for a distance of four or five feet, then there was bare boards up to a high-backed bench, with seats on both sides, almost dividing the room into two parts.

The portion behind the bench was called the snug, this part of the room having some old carpet on the floor and a few seats around a large open fireplace in which a peat fire was glowing. The ceiling was low, with a large beam running across which might have been something of a hazard had it not been for the dividing bench placed strategically under the beam, so that it was only when passing into the snug that you had to mind your head.

About a score of men were drinking beer at the bar and in the snug. They were mostly middle aged, though three or four were quite elderly, and there was an absence of young people; I was certainly the youngest in that evening. The only woman was a middle-aged, rather rotund one behind the bar. She welcomed Bill and Bert in a loud but pleasant voice, and they introduced me to Eileen and her husband Tom.

That first evening in the pub was quite enjoyable as I got to know all the company. Being a new boy I felt I had better stand a round of drinks; fortunately they all drank beer, and at fivepence a pint I had enough money to buy everyone their pint. I also bought four open-top packets of Wild Woodbine cigarettes at twopence for five; I knew I could not afford my usual Gold Flake at a shilling for twenty.

We left the King's Head soon after ten o'clock to return to the bothy, my companions seeming quite happy on the way home. I could count that evening a success now that I had paid my way in, and could feel comfortable in my mind, though I still had my first night away from home before me.

The two foremen shared one of the bedrooms, Arthur was in with me, and Doug had a small room on his own. Taking my candle, I went upstairs, finished the rest of my unpacking and got into a rather hard bed. So much had happened in this one day that it all seemed almost unreal, and I was still pondering on the day's events when Arthur came upstairs, having just returned from the gardens where he had been refuelling the boilers and checking all the glasshouses to make sure that the temperatures were right for the night. He talked at length about the greenhouse duties he had just completed, then he settled down and went to sleep. I found it difficult to get to sleep, perhaps because I was in a strange bed, and my thoughts were on the new life I was about to start.

I could not help thinking of my parents. My father would have a good idea of the kind of life I would now be living, as no doubt he would remember his own bothy days, so I hoped he could assure Mother that I was well able to handle my new position. It was true I was still a bit apprehensive, but I was determined to make a success of my new job. My concern was not so much about the work I was to do in the garden, for I knew my training would stand me in good stead, but I realised I had a lot to learn about living with other men in a bothy. My companions seemed to be quite a good bunch of fellows, so I had hopes of being able to make a success of this too.

We arose at half past five next morning. Arthur lit the fire, boiled a tin kettle and we had a cup of tea, then soon after six o'clock Bill and Arthur set off to the mansion and pleasure gardens, which were about a mile from the bothy. The rest of us went out shortly afterwards to make our way to the glasshouses and kitchen garden,

**A black cooking range took up almost all of one end of the bothy living room – another sketch by Toni Goffe.**

which were just a matter of ten minutes' walking, taking a short cut across a field.

This first morning I was taken round the kitchen garden and the glasshouses by Bert and was shown what was expected of me in my work. The kitchen garden was a little over four acres, sloping away to the south. On the east and west sides were two walls, running down the hill for about a hundred yards. These walls were thatched, with a wide overhang which gave considerable protection from the weather to the many fruit trees trained on wires fixed to both sides of the walls. The trees that clothed the walls were very interesting because of the wide range of fruits: besides apples, pears and plums there were peaches, nectarines, figs, apricots and cherries, with several dozen redcurrants and gooseberries grown on single cordon stems reaching to the top of the ten-foot walls. The land in between was kitchen garden, divided into four by wide pathways, with more fruit trees trained as espaliers on each side of the paths.

On the south side of this garden was a grass orchard in which there were many old, gnarled apple, pear and damson trees. A number of the old apple trees were hosts to large bunches of mistletoe which grew from the trunks and branches in a haphazard fashion; the mistletoe had in some cases been transferred to the younger trained trees in the garden, almost certainly by birds.

The glasshouses on the north side were at the top of the rise and, being in full sun, obtained the maximum light available. There were two ranges of lean-to houses built against a high wall, each of these structures being something over three hundred feet long, and in front were five ninety-foot-span houses together with rows of garden frames, most of which were heated.

Behind the lean-to ranges were two potting sheds with doors through the wall leading directly into the ranges of glass. The two boiler houses were next to the potting sheds, sunk deep into the ground so the hot water could circulate into the greenhouses and frames by convection. All the houses were fitted up with varying numbers of four-inch iron hot-water pipes, but in the frames the pipes were only two inches, so to ensure an easy flow of hot water the delivery pipes at the boilers needed to be six inches in diameter. The plumbing had been arranged to keep the two potting sheds warm so that our plants could be kept comfortable while being potted, this being very important to many of our subjects. The fact that those of us who spent many hours at the potting bench could work in comfort was not a consideration, just a coincidental benefit.

Also behind the wall were three fruit rooms, a mess room, storehouse, tool shed and the Head Gardener's office. At the far end, still behind the wall so as to be out of sight, was a large yard where we stacked our coal in a big open shed. We were using best anthracite, which arrived in very large lumps, and these would crumble if frozen when wet, so all the fuel had to be protected by a cover of straw and timber. This area also served as the stable yard for Peter, the garden horse.

I was given charge of one of the ranges of glass, which was divided into seven houses. There were two peach houses, growing eleven peach trees and four nectarines in varieties which would start to ripen in June and could be cleared by August, when the outdoor trees would continue the season until October. In my vineries I had eight grapevines which ripened in succession from July to December, most of them being black varieties, though I also had two Muscats with very sweet, white fruits. Next door was the fig house, in which each of the two trees would be expected to carry over sixty ripe fruits.

In each of the two carnation houses there were three hundred flowering plants, so I knew that somewhere I would find another six hundred young carnation plants to come into my houses to flower the following year. These young plants would by now have been potted into five-inch pots, and it would almost certainly be my job to put them into their final seven-inch pots in due time.

I was taken into two of the span houses where I was given charge of a wide range of pot plants and ferns. I had now seen all of my charge, which was impressive, but I felt I could manage all I had seen so far.

Next I had to go through the other three span houses, where Bert was the grower. The first two were given over to melons, just over forty plants in all, some still growing and others carrying ripe or nearly ripe fruit, but over half the crop had already been harvested, and begonias were growing in their place. The next-door cucumber house was nearly finished and already given over to some orchids and other tropical plants. This house was still shaded and, being warm and damp, these plants had the environment they needed.

I was introduced to Sid Belmont, a local man who was second journeyman under glass and so had care of the second range of lean-to houses. Again this was divided into sections, with two for tomatoes, and later chrysanthemums, another part taken up by roses growing in beds, and then a long orchard house where fruit trees in pots were forced in the early part of the year. These trees stood outside after fruiting, when the house was given over to growing all kinds of hardy plants in pots for use when decorating

**Lean-to greenhouses, from an old Boulton and Paul catalogue.**

at the mansion. Sid was also concerned with the growing of the many plants in the garden frames.

These were our charges, but it was necessary for us to work with, and for, each other as directed by the foreman, and to make full use of the third journeyman, who had no specific charge of glass, and of the two boys.

Mr. Mills came into the garden soon after eight o'clock. He wanted to be sure I had arrived and had been introduced to my charge. He was a tall, well-dressed man, very erect, with a well-trimmed beard, and when he spoke in a low, kindly voice his whole manner was that of a gentleman, so I found it quite natural to address him as "Sir." He wanted me to know that if I had any real problems I could always make a request to speak to him, but he would not listen to trifles. He told me that he would expect to find my greenhouses always clean and tidy, the tiled floors in the carnation houses scrubbed down daily, and the borders in the fruit houses raked at least twice a week, but daily when the trees were shedding their leaves.

Any tools I might use were to be cleaned and put away as soon as I had finished using them, even if I did require them again later the same day. Mr. Mills then asked me to show him what to do with a rake immediately after use, and here my father's training came in useful. By standing the rake on the end of its handle with the head leaning against a wall I passed one of the basic tests of a gardener, knowing that had I put the rake head downwards anybody stepping on it would force the handle to fly into their face or head with considerable force.

Mr. Mills also impressed on me the absolute necessity of keeping all door handles perfectly clean, as Mr. Morrison's family or their guests would be most annoyed if they soiled their hands or gloves on a dirty door handle when walking through the greenhouses. All the houses had press-down brass handles so that one could open a door with both one's hands full. Using metal polish on these handles, as we did at least twice a week, we had to be particularly careful to ensure that every trace of polish was removed.

It was almost nine o'clock when the Head gave me permission to return to my work, and by then it was time for us to go back to the bothy for our breakfast. "Mum" was already there, having prepared the meal of fried potatoes, egg and bread. It was a rather hurried meal as we had to be back in the garden half an hour later, which meant that Bill and Arthur did not have time to join us for breakfast; Bert said that they could usually scrounge something from the kitchen, so we did not need to worry about them.

We stopped again at one o'clock, but this time we were all together as we had an hour for our dinner. Again "Mum" was there, with a stew of carrots, turnips, potatoes and greens that she had prepared, followed by an apple tart. She stayed with us until we had finished eating, then, when she had done the washing up, her day's work for us was over. Having seen the menu for one day, I felt I could write home that evening and give my parents a good report of this, my first full day in bothy.

Our working day finished at half past five or when it got dark, whichever came first, so I was glad to get back to the bothy just after five o'clock to sum up my first working day at Fonthill House, which, I concluded, had been very satisfactory.

# On the wheel 3

PAY DAY came on Saturday, and my first week at Fonthill had come to an end. At one o'clock everyone lined up outside the Head's office, then in order of preference they went in to draw their wages, giving Mr. Mills a chance to have a word with each of his thirty-one men and boys.

By that time I felt quite settled to bothy life. It was so different from anything I could have imagined. Here was a feeling that did not express itself in words: it was a spirit of togetherness, of wanting to be a unit, and it crept over me so quickly I never noticed it at the time.

This atmosphere, if that is what it was, was not so marked during working hours as we were for a lot of the time with men who lived on the estate or in one of the nearby villages. It was, of course, to everyone's advantage to work together, but outside working hours it seemed right for us to be bothy boys first and part of the community next. At the same time each of us was free to come and go as we pleased, and because of this freedom the bothy door was never locked.

During my third week I did my first duty "on the wheel". Friday evening I took over from Bert, and it was now my turn to do the washing up after tea. I had taken my share of the washing up and of some of the housework at home since I was about ten years old, so neither washing up nor seeing that there was always coal and wood ready for the fires and that the oil lamps were ready and clean was anything new to me.

I had already been instructed in the handling of the greenhouse boilers over the past two weeks, and as these were similar to the boilers in my father's garden I had no problem there. I had attended to the fuelling before I left the garden in the late afternoon, so I knew they would be all right for a few hours.

At half past nine it was time for me to get the greenhouse keys and a hurricane lamp and make my way back to the gardens. First I had to clear the ashes and clinkers from the boilers and refuel them, then I had to go through every house to check the temperature. This had to vary from 45 to 70 degrees F., according to the type of plants growing in the various houses. The fruit houses were kept cool at that time of year, being full of chrysanthemums, while in the orchid and tropical houses the temperature would need to be around 70 degrees.

These temperatures had to be kept steady, no matter how cold or how mild it was outside. We were only allowed a drop or rise of two degrees from late in the evening until morning. Having charge of the boilers both by day and by night, there was no excuse if the temperatures were incorrect. We could have our boilers running fast or slow according to the weather by adjusting the valves to control the flow of hot water.

The Head Gardener would go round all the greenhouses most evenings, and should he find anything not as ordered he would call out the duty man to put things right. This, of course, would mean an interview in the Head's office the next morning at which the offending duty man would be reprimanded, or even severely warned.

Saturdays and Sundays were to the person on duty much like any other working day. He was not usually called upon to do much in the way of growing, although this could happen if the Head so wished. His time was fully occupied watering, opening and closing the ventilators in the greenhouses according to the weather, doing his boiler work—and of course he was always available.

I had to spend that whole week either in the garden or in the bothy where I could be found. Having to do all the chores, it was something of a relief to come "off the wheel". For all this extra work we received an additional payment of three shillings, which was considered ample recompense as what we learnt on duty was discipline and devotion to gardening.

On Tuesdays and Fridays I had to help load into the garden van the many flowering plants and boxes of cut flowers for decorating in the mansion. It was on one of these occasions that I was sent to help and thus saw the big house and the pleasure gardens for the first time. As we approached the drive widened out into a large forecourt, surrounded on three sides by a high stone wall. Here every inch seemed to be covered with well-trained fruit trees interplanted with roses and clematis. The wide stone steps running up to the massive carved doors were a feature of this forecourt, but it was the huge mansion itself which immediately took my attention. It was almost covered with climbing trees and shrubs, some of which must have been over thirty feet high.

Passing through either of the two wrought-iron gates in the forecourt walls one reached the pleasure gardens, which were terraced in keeping with the fall of the land, the terraces varying in width from a few feet to several yards. Some had balustrades around them, others had grass banks falling away to the next level. Yet more had stone or brick surrounds. Steps, grass walks or crazy paving ran down to the lake, which was almost a quarter of a mile from the house. This garden was almost as wide, every inch being cultivated and containing many hundreds of interesting plants, as well as leaving room for masses of bedding plants and countless bulbs.

There were three avenues of small trees running down the terraces, one of variegated holly, another of clipped bay and the third with dwarf crab-apples planted alternately with red and yellow fruits. The crab avenue was at right angles to the house, whilst the other two were at forty-five degrees, giving different vistas to the lake below.

Going down towards the lake there were changes in the plants at each level. Some levels were lawn with flower beds in or around them, others were planted with small shrubs. Then there were heathers, rose gardens, rockeries, groups of herbaceous plants and mixed borders of iris.

Because it was so informal it gave an impression of a glorious muddle, but there was no doubt that it had all been very carefully planned to make the best of a piece of land which could hardly be said to lend itself to the making of a good garden.

The floral decorations inside the mansion were on a grand scale.

Each room had its feature of plants and flowers, and the colour of each of these showpieces had to blend or contrast with the decor of the room. This meant that the Head Gardener would have to know which plants or flowers to grow at various times throughout the year. They would need to fit in with the colour schemes in the many rooms of this huge house at any given moment.

I spent most of my time fetching and carrying for Bert, who, with Bill's help, did most of the floral work under the watchful eye of Mr. Mills. I noticed the way Bert would make the plants fit in with each other. He showed me that almost every plant has a front and at least one side, which could be used to face a display or make the side of any display look natural.

It was fascinating to see the easy way these two men had when handling flowers. They were taken firmly from me, almost carelessly, yet I never saw them damage a single bloom. I learnt to handle cut flowers by firmly holding the base of the stems, which would allow the flower heads to fall slightly apart, thereby reducing rubbing on each other.

We could only move from room to room to do our work when the Butler or the Housekeeper gave us permission, as we were not supposed to come into contact with members of Mr. Morrison's family. We were, of course, working in their private home, so it was not surprising that they were not over keen to see workmen around. We did meet up with them from time to time, and then we were expected to be as unobtrusive as possible and to speak only when spoken to.

Mrs. Morrison was an exception, she would be with us most of the time when we were doing major changes to plants or flowers. It was she who decided what kind of decoration was to be put in any particular place, and before we left she would see that everything was to her satisfaction.

The head housemaid, too, would be interested in our activities. She or one of her girls would be watching to see if we made any mess or spilled any water, and she kept us well supplied with dust-sheets so that we should have no excuse. There were times when one of the housemaids would clear up behind us, and then of course we were blackmailed into giving her some flowers for her bedroom. We did not mind, as really we had pleasure in giving the maids something for themselves. It developed into something of a game; we would drop a petal or a spot of water, then wait to be found out and pay the ransom, often suggesting that this should be paid outside working hours and out of view of others.

The centrepiece on the dining table was changed daily. If a white tablecloth was to be used we would put on flowers of brilliant colours, whereas if the walnut table was not to be covered our display would need to be light colours, perhaps even white, which would reflect in the highly polished surface.

We had, of course, to consult with the Butler as to the flowers we could use so as to fit in with the table he was going to lay. This in turn would decide the size and kind of container we would use for our table decoration. Great care was always necessary, as at times we were using valuable silver or porcelain.

The first few days work in the house was, to some extent, new to me. The size of the operation seemed so great. I was getting a different insight into floral art, something I knew I just had to master, but my experience was making me realise that I had so much to learn.

I had been in the bothy a little over a month when Bert and Bill told me it was time I learnt to do a little poaching; I must take my share of the work to keep the grub score down. At first I protested that it was impossible for me to go out and kill anything, but this approach seemed to have little effect on my mates, so I reminded them that poaching was illegal. Even this did not seem to apply on our estate in the eyes of the other bothy boys, who reminded me that I had already eaten at the past four meals with pheasant as the main dish. We had also eaten rabbit several times during my early weeks, so I had little choice but to accept the invitation to learn how to contribute to our larder.

My first task was to learn my way around this huge estate, which meant long walks through the woods and fields with one or other of my mates. I was being taught a great deal about nature as part of my training. I learnt that rabbits liked to use the same path to and from the feeding grounds, and the little tracks they made through the grass and the woods soon became obvious to me. Those tracks made the little animals vulnerable to predators, including us. I was taught to listen for the squeal of a rabbit attacked by a stoat, to wait for a short time until all went quiet, and then to drive the stoat away and pick up the tender young rabbit that stoats always seem to select.

Having learnt a great deal more about nature, I was introduced to the methods of catching game. At first I found this rather difficult to do, perhaps because I was still a bit squeamish at the thought of killing. Bert was a master of the art of poaching, and as he made even this subject interesting to me so my prejudice gradually disappeared. Bert knew with uncanny accuracy where a bird was squatting or a rabbit sitting. When he saw a rabbit hiding behind a tuft of grass he would place some object such as his coat on the ground for the animal to watch; then, making a detour so as to come up to the animal from behind, he would dive on his prey, all in broad daylight.

All this I had to learn. Often I made mistakes, but slowly I did manage to make some catches. We went out at night looking for the odd pheasant or duck, and I was shown where to expect to find the nests when spring came along. I was told never to take eggs from a duck or pheasant until there were four or five eggs in the nest, and then I was only to take two eggs in a period of three days. That would ensure that the hen kept on laying and did not forsake its nest. We were not too keen on taking from the pheasants or ducks. What we really liked best of all was to find a plover's nest on the open ploughed land. These were not easy to find, as they were little more than a depression in the soil in which the eggs were perfectly camouflaged. We

had no compunction in gathering these eggs, as there was a heavy population of these birds in our area. In any case the number of nests we found was relatively few, so good is nature's way of concealment in the open fields.

The keepers knew we were having some of the game, but just so long as we took only enough for our own needs in the bothy they were not too concerned. They were rearing several thousand birds each year and we were having only two or three a week at most, which meant very little to them, as they in their turn were always looking for something from the garden. We were happy to provide them with what they wanted, so it seemed everyone was quite content with the status quo.

This unofficial and unspoken arrangement extended to the dairyman, who was assured of fruit to go with his cream, while we would be in need of eggs and cream. It was easy to effect the exchange when we got our daily supply of milk.

By these means we kept our grub score down to a low level. Our main source of free food, of course, was the kitchen. Apple pie, meat pie, ham and sometimes bottled fruit found their way to the bothy, while flowers and hothouse fruits were not uncommon in the servants' bedrooms.

So it was that we lived well and cheaply, but we never forgot to look after "Mum", making sure that she lived as well as we did. Without our help she might have found that her widowhood left her very poorly off, as the bothy work was her only source of income. She made great efforts to repay us in many little ways; our socks were darned, buttons sewn on and our clothes mended. A great deal of our personal washing was done, too, more often than not without an exchange of words. I often wondered if we did these things for "Mum" from a selfish angle, but we did have a deep affection for her and I like to think this was the main reason for our helping her.

# Alarms and excursions 4

WE WERE all in the bothy one evening in November when a gale blew up. The wind seemed to get stronger as the evening went on, and around eight o'clock we heard a crash as a large tree blew down. When we went out to investigate we found it was rather too close to the bothy for comfort. We were looking at the fallen tree when Arthur saw another leaning in our direction, so we made a run for it, just getting clear before it gave way to the wind pressure and came crashing down.

By that time we were really alarmed. The bothy was surrounded by trees, and there was a real risk of one falling on to the roof. Bert took charge of the situation, telling us to put on as many clothes as we could wear and get out of the bothy, staying out until he thought it was safe to return.

We were only too happy to do as our foreman told us. Having got us all outside, Bert went back in, first to put out the fires and then to douse the oil lamps to make sure there would be no fire if our home was damaged by falling timber. It was good to know that we had a man in charge who was keeping very calm and taking the necessary precautions.

We waited under the shelter of a hedge for some time, with the wind seeming to get even stronger. We saw two more trees uprooted as we sheltered there. Then Bert decided we must all go to the garden to see if there was any damage to the glasshouses and to do anything we could do to prevent further damage. It was a frightening experience, because glass was being ripped out from the houses and garden frame lights were being lifted from their frames and blown down into the kitchen garden. We tried to hold some of these lights down with sacks of potatoes, but so strong was the wind that the heavy bags were rolled off as the wind got under the glass.

Then the Head Gardener took over. He took one look and told

everyone to get well away, giving strict orders that no-one was to go into or near any of the houses, as a great deal of glass was flying around. Large elm and lime trees were being blown as much as fifty feet by the wind, and had any of us been near the lean-to ranges we could well have been badly cut. In the fitful moonlight we could see devastation all around, but there was nothing anybody could do while the gale was at its height.

By four o'clock in the morning Mr. Mills decided it would be safe for us to return to the bothy. The gale had just about blown itself out and, the night being mild, our Head said we had better leave everything until the morning, when we would be able to see what we were doing and to avoid getting cut on the broken glass. We found our bothy undamaged, except for a number of slates missing from the roof, so we were able to get to bed for an hour or so.

Next day everyone was employed gathering up barrowfuls of broken glass. This was a job that needed great care, not only to avoid getting cut but also to find every small piece; any left on or in the ground would be a hazard when planting at a later date.

The old lean-to ranges had lost a great deal of glass, and it was here that we had our greatest losses. The span houses, being somewhat lower, were more or less intact. Most of the grapes still hanging in the vineries had to be destroyed as they had been damaged by flying glass, while a considerable number of chrysanthemums and carnations were ruined, as well as most of our stock of geraniums. The roses, and the fig and peach trees, were not too badly hurt, and a surprising number of our pot plants survived. We moved all we could from the lean-to ranges into the span houses, and there they had to stay until repairs could be done by the estate maintenance staff.

Those repairs could not start for several days, as the roads and drives on the estate had first to be cleared of fallen trees and branches. We learnt later that an estimated thousand trees had been lost on our estate, and that meant the four foresters had two years' work ahead of them clearing up and replanting.

Mr. Morrison gave orders that for each tree that was lost three young ones of the same kind were to be planted. This presented no problems for our foresters, for it seemed they raised many hundreds of seedling trees every year to make good the loss of trees that were harvested in the normal course of events. This harvesting and planting was something I had never even thought about, but I could see it was good husbandry. To the foresters it was as normal as planting and harvesting any other crop.

It was late December before all our greenhouses were repaired. By moving plants into each house as it was put in order we were able to save quite a lot of our stock, and at the same time we maintained a reasonable flow of fruit and flowers into the mansion.

One of the storm casualties that took some time to replace was our little weather station. Not only did we lose a thermometer but we lost our wind-speed gauge, which was doubly unfortunate as without that instrument we never knew just how strong the wind had been that night. At our weather station we recorded the daily minimum and maximum temperatures with a thermometer in a small box-like structure with louvred sides which allowed air to flow past the thermometer, giving a true reading. The daily rainfall was taken by measuring and recording the amount of rainwater collected in a glass container below a five-inch funnel, and the hours of sunshine, the atmospheric pressure and the wind direction were also recorded. All this enabled us to act as a weather sub-station for the Meteorological Office.

Christmas was a busy time for everyone. There was to be a banquet and ball for the county people on the evening of Boxing Day, and the whole house had to be decorated with plants and flowers. Garlands of holly were to be draped around the ballroom, and of course it was our task to make these garlands. As they had to be the correct length for the position in which they were to hang we made them in the ballroom, and this meant working late into the evenings.

At least it gave me a chance to see this magnificent room, with its beautiful fireplace of white marble. Carvings of trees supported the mantelshelf, the wrought-iron fire basket was backed by a black metal plate embossed with a cedar tree, and the fire irons, set in a marble fender, were of burnished steel with ivory handles. The gilt overmantel matched the walls of white and gold, and all this contrasted so well with the ceiling which was painted to resemble an evening sky with the stars just beginning to appear.

The foresters had brought a large Christmas tree to the front door, and it fell to us to carry it into the ballroom and to set it up at one end of the room in a large wooden barrel. Then we had to dress it overall and fix Christmas candles into small holders set on the branches. A candle snuffer on a long cane was provided, and a bucket of water was placed nearby with a small garden syringe ready for use should a candle set alight to a part of the tree. All these activities had to be finished by three o'clock in the afternoon of Christmas Eve, when everyone had to assemble outside the front door.

It was as we assembled there that I realised the number of people employed on the estate. Gathered together in the forecourt were the farmhands, the gamekeepers, the foresters, the chauffeurs, the maintenance men, the gardeners, including "Mum", and the outdoor staff, in fact everyone who worked on the estate. In order of status we were called to meet Mr. Morrison and his lady, and each of us was given a present of money varying according to his place in the hierarchy of his particular department. For my part, I received five shillings, and this was given as a crown piece.

By this means Mr. and Mrs. Morrison met everyone once a year. This was, to us, supposed to be a great honour; I am afraid the pleasure of meeting our employer wore a bit thin that day, having to wait outside on a cold, damp afternoon for over an hour.

On Boxing Day there was to be a shoot, and Mr. Morrison invited some of his guests to take part. Over a hundred men from the estate, including four of us from the bothy, and some of the unemployed men from the villages were detailed to go as beaters. Our first job was to work our way in a line through the woods, beating the bushes and undergrowth to drive the pheasants and any other game before us, so getting the birds to fly over the guns.

The seven keepers had been raising the game throughout the spring and summer. The birds had then been released in the woods and fed there, so the keepers knew where they were to be found.

The Head Gamekeeper was in charge of the shoot, so it was he or one of his men who told us what we had to do. What did surprise us was that he was also in charge of the guns, telling them where they had to stand and when to be there.

We beaters assembled at eight in the morning, then had a two-mile walk to a place called Fire Wood, where we were lined up for the first drive. Each man was supposed to be about ten yards from his neighbour, with a keeper on either flank and two other keepers amongst us to try to keep everyone in a straight line, and if necessary to turn one or the other flank to a prearranged plan. It took us nearly an hour to work our way through this wood, driving many birds, rabbits, hares and a few deer before us. When we did clear the wood there were the guns, ten of them, shooting at everything that moved.

Each of the men shooting had two or even three guns, and a loader was at hand to keep at least one gun loaded at all times. When the beaters came out into the clearing and there was nothing else moving to shoot at, that was the end of the first drive. There must have been about eighty dead pheasants lying around, as well as a lot of rabbits and some hares. I also saw, for the first time, a dead woodcock.

Two men brought in a shot deer. To me this was not a pretty sight, but it was part of my job, so I with the others had to go with the keepers to start on the second drive. This time we did not have far to walk, to a place called Middle Leys. Again we were lined up, then, as before, we drove through the wood, only this time we had to clamber through brambles and bracken, which made progress rather slow, much to the annoyance of the keepers, who tried to hurry us as it was considered bad service to keep the gentry waiting.

After a certain amount of coaxing, and at the price of many bruises and scratches, we eventually beat our way through to another clearing. Here the guns were waiting for the second shoot, and again there were many dead birds lying around, with dogs bringing in wounded game.

Around midday Jim arrived with the garden van, bringing lunch for the beaters. There were meat sandwiches, cheese and beer. We stood around eating for a time, then loaded all the dead game into the van. Meanwhile the guns with their loaders and some lady guests who had arrived to watch the shooting retired to a nearby shooting lodge to enjoy a hot luncheon brought from the mansion by motorvan. This gave time for the beaters to start another drive before the guns needed to take up their position. Altogether there were five drives that day, the last finishing a little before four o'clock, and then the bag had to be counted.

More than three hundred pheasants, dozens of rabbits and hares, two woodcock and two deer had lost their lives, and everyone seemed happy with the day's work. Everything was loaded into Jim's van and taken back to the game larder for hanging or until they were sold.

The guns, the loaders and the ladies were taken back to the mansion in two motorvans called shooting brakes, but we had almost three miles to walk before we were back at the bothy. We were tired and hungry, and were glad to find that Bill, who was duty man, had tea ready for us. That was just as well, as the day was far from over for us.

Having eaten, washed and changed our clothes, we were to be at the mansion in the evening to help in the kitchen with the washing up. This, apparently, was part of the bargain between the kitchen girls and the bothy boys. We knew it would be well worth our while to keep our part of the bargain.

As we passed into the forecourt we could see four horse-drawn carriages and a number of motorcars in which more guests had arrived for the dinner and ball. This was a grand affair, with a seven-course meal served in the grand dining room where, we understood, there were sixty-six sitting at table. To judge from the washing up there seemed to us to be many more than that!

Guests were still arriving late into the evening for the dancing, which went on until after three in the morning. We were kept busy most of the time, but even so it was an enjoyable time for us "below stairs". We had plenty to eat and drink, and for the first time I had a glass of champagne and tasted caviar.

I got to know most of the indoor staff, of whom I had met three of the six housemaids before. It was a special pleasure to meet the three girls from the kitchen who worked under the Cook, who was also in charge of the two stillroom maids who did most of the pastry and cake making. They needed to be highly skilled in the art of decorating the marvellous dishes they produced.

We saw very little of the Butler or of his two footmen, as they were serving the guests throughout the evening, and it was left to the Cook and the Housekeeper to see that we did our work properly and with care. As the night wore on, however, neither of them seemed to notice, or to care, that we were all enjoying ourselves. The work had to go on, all the same, and the first kitchen maid, keeping a clear head, saw to it that we did the job to her satisfaction.

A great number of silver dishes came back to us, and these had to be washed one by one in a wooden sink to avoid scratching the surface of the silver. Even greater care had to be used when washing the delicate and sometimes valuable china and porcelain, which were again washed separately and in wooden sinks. The glasses were taken to the Butler's pantry and there washed by the stillroom maids. The hot water was on tap from a small boiler which had to be kept going on full draught to supply all the water that we needed. It was most intriguing to be able to use hot water from a running tap.

It was in the not-so-early hours that we returned to the bothy, bringing with us enough Christmas fare to last us for several days. We were all so glad to go to bed after such a long, hard day, but we could have only two hours sleep as the next day was an ordinary working day and we had to be on the job at six-thirty.

The weather turned very cold in January and ice formed on the lake. Now this was very important, and presented an opportunity that could not be missed. Each morning while the frost lasted three or four of us were sent to the lake to collect ice. It was a cold, wet job. First of all we had to break the ice, then we drew the ice to the side of the lake using long poles with an attached iron hook, trying to keep the ice as clean as possible. Jim would be there with his horse and cart, and we would load him up with all the ice we could get so he could take it to the icehouse to be stored.

The icehouse was situated in a nearby wood where it was cool even in summer; the site chosen was a north-facing bank, into which a tunnel was dug running slightly downwards. This entrance was about four feet high and the same in width; the tunnel was about six feet long and opened out into a room ten feet square, dropping some nine feet below the level of the tunnel floor. The room and the tunnel were both brick lined, with iron joists supporting the roof, and in the middle of the stone floor was a drain to take away any surplus water. At both ends of the entrance tunnel there were solid iron doors, making the tunnel into the necessary air trap.

We would try to get a ton of ice each day, a good deal more if it was available. The ice was shovelled down into the icehouse and left to settle into a solid block under its own weight. Later it would be covered with a thick layer of straw to act as insulation. We would, of course, add to the heap as more ice became available, so that by the end of the winter the icehouse would probably be full of a solid block of ice. At first I was surprised to be told that this would keep as ice right through to the following summer, but this did not seem so strange when I went back later to add more ice and found the temperature inside very cold indeed.

Although it was the gardeners' job to get the ice and to store it away, for some strange reason it was the keepers' task to dig some out with icepicks once or twice a week in the summer for use in the kitchen ice boxes, this being the only means of refrigeration in the mansion at that time.

Ice was also needed in the Butler's pantry and in the dining room to cool the wine, so at least one cellaret was always at hand. These containers, sometimes very elaborate in design, were usually made of mahogany or oak and were lined with lead. They would hold anything from four to ten bottles of wine, surrounded by ice. This was all very interesting, but not very efficient in these modern times, so it was not altogether surprising that this was to be a year of considerable change.

Mr. Morrison decided to install electricity in the mansion. First, an engine house was built a short distance from the house—the distance minimised the effect of noise—and a new petrol engine was put in to charge the many glass accumulators that were lined up side by side and connected to each other in what was called the new battery house. From these accumulators direct current was fed to the many rooms in the mansion by cable and wire, providing both light and power. Not only did this mean the end of gas lighting in the "Big House" but a new refrigerator was bought for the kitchen, which meant that we would no longer use the ice house.

Up to this time the maintenance men had been in charge of the gas house, where there was an exchanger which fed water on to carbide to make acetylene gas which was stored in a large gas-holder, rather like a small-scale town gas supply. The gas was fed under pressure along small-bore pipes to all the gas lamps in the mansion. These gave a strong, white light, but there was always a risk of fire.

It was this risk that led to those of us who lived in the bothy as well as a few other men who lived nearby being detailed to train as firemen. From time to time a fire bell was sounded, and as soon as we heard this we had to drop everything and run or cycle to the mansion, man the fire hoses and be ready to fight a fire. Not that our equipment amounted to very much; we had ten fire hoses on reels to join together if needed, and these were connected to one of the four standpipes that were strategically placed around the mansion.

We would have to place at least two ladders against the first-floor windows as a means of escape, but anyone on the top floor had to escape by means of a canvas chute. This was a long tube about two feet wide; one end was fixed to a wooden frame placed inside up against the window frame, and the other end would be thrown out of the window. Anyone using this chute would sit on the window ledge with their feet inside the chute, then slide into the chute and down to the ground, keeping steady by pushing the feet and elbows outward; it was surprising how one could lower oneself little by little using this method. All the same, two of us on the ground would have to man the lower end of the chute and pull it outwards to try to keep the whole length at an angle of about forty-five degrees so as to steady the descent of the person coming down. We would have to get them out quickly and be ready for others who needed to escape.

Not surprisingly, perhaps, this method of escape was most unpopular with the inside staff, but at times we would persuade somebody to make the effort. Everyone who was inside the house had to co-operate, and they had to get out as quickly as possible using only those ways of escape that were deemed not to be on fire.

All these activities were planned and directed by a fire expert who was employed to come at any time to raise the alarm and to train us and the indoor staff in fire drill. He would note how long we took to assemble, to take up our positions on the end of the chute and to be ready to turn on the water. Of course, we were never quick enough, so we never received any praise, nor for that matter did we receive any money for these extra duties.

Garden Engine.

# Friends and poachers 5

AS TIME went by I came to know almost all of the people who lived in our village and in the other two nearby villages. There were a few men who had cars and worked away from the district, but most of the people got their living from the land or worked on the estates doing the many jobs that had to be done, usually with considerable skill. We in the bothy were accepted by the local people as land workers; even so, the feeling that we were foreigners was never far below the surface.

This was more obvious with the young men, partly because we usually had a little more money in our pockets but mainly because of the village girls. Some of them were interested in us simply because we were new faces, but we were interested in them because they were girls. There was often a touch of rivalry between us and the village lads, and that did lead to trouble on occasions. Sometimes it even led to blows. We in the bothy always closed ranks if it became necessary; to us it seemed the proper thing to do as we were in many ways brothers in a family.

This rivalry came over to some extent in the village reading room which was, in fact, a kind of youth club where we played games in the winter evenings. This was open to all young men. Why the girls were excluded no one really knew; perhaps it was felt that it was unladylike for girls to play games. There came a time when four of us from the bothy were winning more than our fair share of games at the reading room, and we were distinctly unpopular for a time. A move was made to keep the bothy boys out on the grounds that we were not local people, but fortunately for us the matter was resolved by the parish council decreeing that we should be allowed to continue membership.

It so happened that there were nine villages in the area all having their own reading rooms where table tennis, darts, dominoes, shove-ha'penny and card games were played. The villages formed a kind of inter-village league to play these games on Monday evenings on a home-and-away basis; competition was always keen and we enjoyed these evenings, so it was no hardship having to cycle as much as eight miles for our away games.

I was pleased to find there were two other estates in the area where there was a garden bothy, and we met the men from these bothies playing in these village games. The fact that we were all bothy boys made us firm friends, and it seemed that every bothy had the same kind of local problems. These men came from various parts of the country and had worked on estates in many different counties, and their company and their conversation was extremely interesting. I was beginning to learn something of the fraternity of the bothies and was gleaning a lot of information about other estates, about the strength of the garden staff, what was being grown and, most important, the personality of the Head Gardener. All this information, I felt, might serve me well later on.

Every Friday evening during the winter months we would go to the village dance, held in an old army hut which served as a village hall. The Lord of the Manor had given permission for the hut, bought by the village people for ten pounds, to be erected by them on common land.

Just about everyone went to these sixpenny hops, at which we danced to the music of a piano, violin and drums. The dances were always a mixture of modern and old-time, the Charleston and the quickstep being popular, along with the lancers, barn dance, polka and veleta. All ages were represented; among the older dancers were grandparents who came with their children and grandchildren, all joining in the evening's fun together. The older people taught us younger ones many of the old-time dances.

Those were happy evenings, but we felt it was a great pity that the girls from the manor were not allowed out during the dark evenings. Much pleading to the Housekeeper made no difference, and our offer to act as escorts was firmly turned down.

The other villages in the district also had their weekly dances and social evenings, so when off duty there was no need for us to spend many evenings in the bothy if we had enough money to go out. Money was, of course, always in short supply, so the question was raised of our doing some evening work privately in one or two of the smaller gardens nearby.

Bert was not too happy with the idea; he told us not to do anything until he'd asked Mr. Mills if he had any objections. The Head Gardener objected very strongly: if we had any time to spare, he said, he would find work for idle hands! Then he asked if we were complaining about our money. Bert, ever the diplomat, told him we were all well satisfied, which was straining the truth to the limit.

As winter gave way to spring our work in the garden became harder, yet more interesting. Everything seemed to be in a hurry; just as soon as the daylight started to increase so our plants seemed to spring into action. The fruit trees under glass were safe enough, but those on the outside of the walls needed to be covered at night with rolls of hessian when in flower if there was the slightest risk of frost. There was little we could do about the apple, pear and plum trees, so the spring frosts acted as an agent to do our fruit thinning for us; all the time we were hoping that the trees were not being thinned too much.

Great quantities of vegetables were now coming from the forcing pits and greenhouses. Rhubarb, sea kale, chicory and endive could now be supplied daily to the kitchen, along with early cucumbers, lettuces, spring onions and tomatoes. There was now so much to do during the day and after tea that we no longer gave any thought to the idea of working for other people in the evenings.

This was also the time of year when we in the bothy bought some new clothes for best and to take our seconds for work. We were expected always to be reasonably well dressed, because from time to time we would have to meet the gentry in the course of our duties.

Almost all our clothes were bought at the door. From time to time a travelling salesman called at the bothy, offering all the clothes we might possibly need. He carried a large selection of clothes of all kinds, and he took great care to see that we were well satisfied with everything we bought. His prices were below ordinary retail prices; he was able to sell a good shirt for three shillings and sixpence (17½p) and a suit cost two pounds five shillings (£2.25). He took orders for the suits for a firm in Leeds. They were "off-the-peg" but he did measure us to make sure they were a reasonable fit when they arrived later by post. We aimed to buy one new suit each year if we could afford to do so.

The salesman was welcome for another reason. As he called on many bothies on his rounds he was able to keep us informed on the movement of men and to tell us of the jobs that might become available over a large part of the west of England.

We also had calling on us a boot and shoe salesman, whom we saw about three times a year. He too was a great provider of news from the estates in the southern counties.

It was necessary for us to wear an apron during working hours, not only to keep our clothes clean but because the status of the servant demanded the wearing of an apron. I was now able to discard my old green apron and to wear a blue serge one, partly due to a change in fashion but mainly because I was now a first journeyman and was not required to wear a green one any more. In my position I was expected to wear a collar and tie.

It was about this time that I was able to get a place in the local football team. When not on duty I was playing every Saturday afternoon, and I was always pleased when we played away from home as we travelled in motor cars, something rather unusual for those of us who worked on the land. Everyone was keen to get picked for these games, even if it did cost us an extra ninepence.

It was playing football that I first met up with Eli Dheon. He was one of a large family of gipsies and one of the most friendly people it has been my good fortune to meet. The family had a small-holding, and from the age of twelve everyone worked on the land, the girls as well as the boys.

Joseph Dheon, the father, had a Renault coach-type car and Eli had bought himself a new Morris Cowley. They were the only two-car family in the district, apart from the gentry, and it was in these two cars that we went to our away football matches.

The Dheon boys sometimes hired themselves out to the local

farmers on a day-to-day basis; they all seemed to be able to do almost any job on the farm from hoeing and haymaking to harvesting and hedgelaying. Laying hedges required great skill to cut halfway through the growing young timbers of an old hedge, carefully laying each piece down in a horizontal position. They were all laid the same way to make an impenetrable hedge, at the same time making sure the cut timbers were not cut so far through that they would die.

It was a strange fact that everyone trusted the Dheons, even though it was clear to everyone that they made their living mainly by poaching. This fact was well known to our gamekeepers, and a constant battle of wits went on between the Dheons and the keepers on our estate. They were caught on occasions and prosecuted in the courts; they always pleaded guilty, and were happy to pay any fine as part of their normal living expenses.

One day Eli, not being too careful, was caught by Mr. Morrison himself. It appears that the conversation that followed went something like this:

Mr. Morrison: "What do you think you're doing stealing my rabbits?"
Eli: "They're not your rabbits, they're wild ones."
Mr. Morrison: "They are mine, and they're on my land."
Eli: "That doesn't prove they are yours, but what I will do, sir, if ever I find one with your name on it I'll bring it round to you straight away."
Mr. Morrison: "All right, Eli, you do that."
Eli: "Well then, if you'll excuse me, sir, I must start at once looking for your rabbits."
Mr. Morrison: "You win this time, Eli, but if I ever catch you on my land again I'll prosecute."

For a time nobody really believed this story, but some months later Mr. Morrison told this tale when making an after-dinner speech. It was our turn to apologise to Eli for our disbelief.

I came to respect this family, for they lived a clean, healthy life and were always willing to help others. This was demonstrated when, during a spell of very cold weather, all the taps in the village street were frozen. The water from those taps was the only water available to most of the people, so it was vital to get the water thawed as quickly as possible. It was the Dheon boys who had the water running each morning well before seven o'clock. Nobody had asked them for this help; they just did it for the good of the village. They themselves got no benefit from their efforts as they always used spring water from a pump.

It so happened that one of these mornings around daybreak the gamekeepers saw a man poaching. They were unable to catch him as he quickly drove away in a car. The keepers were quite sure that it was Eli's car, so they took out a summons against him.

This time Eli pleaded not guilty. In court the two keepers said that it was Eli they saw poaching, but two village people gave evidence that it could not have been him as he was at that time helping to get the village taps running.

It was clear that a Morris Cowley was used at the scene of the poaching incident, so Eli was found guilty and fined, much to the disgust of some of the local people. There was talk of an appeal, but Joseph being very much the head of the family would have nothing to do with what he called making further trouble; he just wanted the matter forgotten.

Eli told us later that it was his father who was rabbiting that morning. As it was his father who always paid the fines, perhaps justice was done after all.

# Work and play 6

THE HOME FARM was a very important part of the estate, and this was managed by the Farm Bailiff who had equal standing with our Head Gardener in the hierarchy on the estate.

The farm was mainly given over to dairy farming, with a herd of about eighty cows, and perhaps as many as three hundred laying hens and some cockerels. Then there were fifty or more turkeys and some ducks. Anything up to thirty porkers and bacon pigs were kept in a brick enclosure with sleeping pens down one side.

Some of the output from the farm was sent to market, but quite a large part of the produce went to the mansion as milk, cream, butter, eggs, cheese, pork and chicken.

Under the Bailiff's supervision, the dairyman had two men and two women working for him. It was by making sure that these ladies were never short of fruit and flowers that we in the bothy ensured we were kept fairly well supplied with dairy produce.

With the coming of summer an innovation was seen in the fields, a long portable shed divided into sections with tubes running the whole length. This, we were informed, was a milking machine, something I had never seen before. It was driven by the power takeoff from a tractor. A small area was surrounded with hurdles, and into this the cows were driven. Five at a time, they were pushed into cubicles in the shed and their teats were connected to the milking machine, and at the same time they were fed with cow cake. When they had been milked and fed, they walked out of their cubicles into the field, and five others took their place.

It really was surprising how quickly the animals got used to this new method of milking. Much time was saved as there was no longer any need to drive the herd to the dairy twice a day. There were some teething problems with the machine at first, usually because the dairymen were not used to handling that kind of equipment, but when they got accustomed to it the machine seemed to work very well.

The same easing of the work on the farm was seen in the hay field as tractors took over from horses. Hay sweeps were fitted to the front of the tractors and the hay was swept from the fields direct to the ricks; the hay was lifted on to the stack by elevator driven from the tractor's power takeoff. Ploughing, too, began to be done almost entirely by tractor, which was able to cut three furrows at a time, getting the job done much quicker than could a pair of horses cutting only one furrow.

Things were indeed changing very fast on the farm, and we in the gardens were very interested to see such dramatic developments. We were also a little envious, as all our work still had to be done by hand and, now that the days were longer, we were having to work an extra half an hour each day for twelve weeks to make up for the time lost during the past winter, when it had been too dark for work at half-past four.

We received no extra pay for this work or for any other overtime that we might be called on to do. We in the bothy were at a distinct disadvantage when it came to overtime as the Head could call upon us at any time to do anything he thought necessary. Very often he did have us doing jobs, especially on Sunday mornings when he could make a point of reminding us just how well we were being trained, and what a splendid thing it was for us to be so well disciplined.

I suppose we were lucky that Mr. Mills was rather keen on sport because that meant he encouraged us to play games by not calling on us to do any overtime on Saturday afternoons. He himself was very keen on cricket and played for the estate team most Saturdays. This was very fortunate for me as this was the game I most enjoyed.

There were four of us in the bothy who could hold our places in the team: Bert was very useful behind the stumps, Bill usually opened the batting and Arthur could bowl quite fast, while I was able to make some runs and come on as a change bowler. It was in the fielding that I felt at my best. It was seldom the four of us were able to play together as when it was our turn on garden and bothy duty we could have no time for games; our work had to come before anything.

It was most fortunate for us on the estate that Mr. Morrison too was happy to see his employees playing games, and it was he who paid for most of the equipment we used. He gave us grants from time to time, and when he made two grass tennis courts available it was decided to form a sports club to incorporate tennis, cricket and football. This was a new project and at first nobody really knew how to get it off the ground, but with a thirty-pound gift from our employer we were soon the envy of the surrounding villages. We had two tennis courts and a separate cricket ground and a football pitch.

We knew that in course of time our neighbours would also get similar facilities from their squire, because there seemed to be a sense of rivalry between the squires of the various villages. This was, of course, to the benefit of the workers; no lord of the manor could be seen to neglect his manor.

One major change on our estate was the making of a new water garden on the lakeside. Small shallow, meandering canals were dug in some woodland at the top end of the lake and little bridges were built over them, then the whole area was planted with many hundreds of primulas and other water-loving plants.

The lower end of the lake was a great attraction to some of us. It was very deep in places and ducks made their nests on the water's edge. Although we were not supposed to swim in it, in the latter part of the summer evenings we would go to a wooded part of the lakeside and have our swim, making sure we could not be seen from the house.

This was fine for two seasons, and then one of our friends from the village got into difficulties with cramp. We managed to save him from drowning, but it was a near thing and it put us off for a time.

It was fortunate for us that it did put us off our swimming, because about a week later a body was taken from the water. One of our keepers spotted something in the lake, got out a boat to investigate, and then called in the village constable. With help they managed to get the dead man out of the water; apparently he had been at the bottom of the lake for a long time, and we had been swimming in that water only a few days before.

The discovery of that body caused a good deal of trouble, as no one knew who he was. We thought it politic to remain silent about our swimming there in case we were called to the inquest, which failed to resolve the mystery of the man's identity.

Arthur and I were sorry about this incident for another reason. He and I had been training for many weeks and we had planned to ask permission to swim the length of the lake, which was a little over a mile. We both felt we could have done it, but now the chance never came to give ourselves that satisfaction.

It became almost a habit with us when not on duty to go to our neighbouring village on Sunday evenings during the summer and call in at the *Fellowship and Rest*, an old thatched inn with flagstone floors that were always covered with a layer of sawdust. There were a few wooden seats, showing signs of wear by constant use over the years, and a number of spittoons were placed on the floor at intervals; those seats seemed to belong to certain elderly men as if by right.

The house was timber framed, and all the old beams were visible, both inside and out. The so-called bar at one end of the main room was little more than a table with barrels of beer on the bench behind and, above the barrels, a shelf with a few bottles of wine, whisky and gin. The bar room was long and narrow, with a bay window at one end; an old Valor oil heater and three oil lamps kept the place warm and gave a reasonable light.

There was an outer room through which one passed to get to the bar, but it was almost bare of furniture and rather cold. That room was only used during the summer days when a lot of people came in, and when that happened there was a scramble for the half-dozen beer barrels which served as seats.

At first sight one might have felt the whole place could do with a good clean-up and a coat of paint, but on reflection one realised that might have been the one thing to have spoilt the homely atmosphere of the old pub. The landlord fitted in perfectly; he had a long white beard, somewhat stained with beer and snuff.

No one knew his age—not even he himself, so he said. He was a great storyteller, telling tales mainly about his life at sea, and he assured us that all his lies were true. He would tell the most outrageous stories about his young wife, who took it all with considerable grace. Although he must have been getting on in years he was a very happy man, and his loud, infectious laughter even at his own tales was something we all loved to hear.

The house was very popular with almost everyone living nearby, both men and women. On Sunday evenings in the summer there was dancing on the stones outside to a melodeon played by Old Tom; it went on until about nine o'clock, by which time Old Tom was usually a bit under the weather.

It was on one of these Sundays that I met a girl who, rightly or wrongly, had something of a reputation. There were four of us from the bothy enjoying the company with some other fellows and girls when our Head Gardener passed by just at the moment I was dancing with the girl in question. None of us gave the matter any thought, so I was very surprised when the following morning I was called into Mr. Mills' office. The Head left me in no doubt that he disapproved of the company I was keeping, and I was given a lecture on morals. Not only that, he told me that I would be sent home if I was seen in the girl's company again. It was made very clear to me that I was in his charge at all times, not only during working hours.

When August came Mr. Morrison and all the family went to Scotland for the grouse shooting, together with the Butler, one footman, the Cook and two housemaids. Our garden had to supply vegetables, fruit, cut flowers and flowering plants to the house in Scotland for the ten weeks the family were there.

Every week we would pack a hamper of vegetables and fruit and one or two boxes of cut flowers, and every third week we would send a box of flowering plants, fuschias, hydrangeas, Michaelmas daisies, chrysanthemums, coleus, geraniums and ferns, all growing in pots. The plants were packed tightly into boxes and then a kind of small wigwam was built over them to ensure their safe transit by rail to Scotland. As none of these plants were ever returned it was part of our job to propagate more for future years.

The Royal Horticultural Society's fruit and vegetable show, open to all of the United Kingdom, was held in London during October. Many of the large estates compete at this major show and competition was very keen, so only the very best was good enough to be exhibited. The prestige of the garden was, to some extent, at stake.

We had started to prepare our fruit and vegetables months before the show date. Onions and leeks had been sown under glass in January and potted on as they grew; the onions were planted outside in April in well-manured beds, and the leeks were set out in trenches. We had drilled deep holes in the ground and filled them with fine soil in which to sow our parsnips and carrots, while celery and cauliflowers had been started in the glasshouses, then planted out in season.

The potatoes were planted in plots of ground where most of the stones had been removed, to make sure the tubers were not disfigured. A great deal of peat was added to the soil when we planted them. The tomatoes, lettuces, cucumbers and melons were started a little later so as to be at their best in early October. These, and many other vegetables, were carefully tended, fed and watered as necessary to ensure top quality.

Every one of us in the garden from the Head down was only too keen to do anything at any time to make sure that we were going to show the very best; time and effort counted for nothing. All this enthusiasm stemmed from Mr. Mills; everyone had his full confidence, which gave us all the encouragement we needed.

He would show us how to get more natural colour on apples by removing some leaves to expose the fruits to dew and sunshine. This we also did to the peaches and nectarines. We were shown how to handle plums and grapes to keep the bloom on these, the most delicate of fruits, and we were shown how with a match we could lift the old calyx on apple and pears so that each of the segments was erect and undamaged. The long parsnips and carrots were lifted without bruising by flooding each plant with water. These and many other ideas well worth knowing for the show bench were ours for the asking or for the watching.

Most of the pears, apples, peaches, plums, apricots, nectarines and figs were grown on the trained trees on the thatched walls. There they could be protected from the birds by nets and, in the case of pears, by muslin bags. The fruit had been put in these bags, which were tied to the trees, in early August, so it was fully protected from birds and strong sunlight.

By September much of our fruit and vegetables had been selected, and some had been gathered in. This process continued right up to the weekend before the show, when Mr. Mills made his final selection, the melons and grapes being the last. Everything was then carefully packed in specially made boxes for the trip to London by train.

Mr. Mills took his three foremen with him, travelling up with the exhibits early on Monday morning. They needed two taxis to get the boxes across London to Vincent Square, where the show was held. For the rest of the day and on into the evening they were staging our vegetables and fruit; they could continue doing this up to ten o'clock on Tuesday morning, when everything had to be ready for judging.

With the Head Gardener and his foremen all in London, I was left in charge of the gardens for three days. For the first time I realised the responsibility and the amount of work the Head Gardener had to undertake. It was fortunate I was not "on the wheel" during the week as I had so many things to attend to; I doubt if I could have managed to do a duty week as well.

I had to make sure the needs of the mansion were supplied. Fruit, flowers and vegetables had to be taken as required and the dining table centrepiece had to be changed daily. It was for me to see that the men were at their jobs on time. The Head had given me a full list of duties for the men before he went away, but even so I gained a lot of experience during those few days.

It was very enjoyable having the responsibility of running the garden for a few days, yet I was not sorry when Wednesday evening came and I could relax a little. It seemed our Head was well satisfied with the show results, and if he was happy that meant we had done well in London.

Twenty-one prize cards were added to the near three hundred displayed in the Head's office. We were invited in to see the prizes we had helped to win. In pride of place were the eleven First Prize cards. The Head was pleased to say all went well in the garden on his return, and I knew this was praise indeed from a man of few words.

He was also a man with a sense of humour. He was highly amused one day when he saw a young lad in the orchard scrumping apples and he called out "Where do you think you're going, Robert?" Back came the reply "I ain't going nowhere, Mr. Mills, I be coming back." This little story he told many times, but he never forgot young Robert; I gathered that later Robert was taken into the garden as a garden boy, and was quickly made up to a journeyman and installed into the bothy, which was rather unusual for a local boy.

Another incident that showed us his character and judgment occurred when the kitchen garden foreman was picking damsons and put several pounds into his own dinner bag to take home. Unfortunately for him Mr. Mills had seen him do it, and when the opportunity offered the Head removed the bag from the messroom and took it, with the damsons inside, into his own office. He then sent for the foreman to confront him with the stolen fruit.

Most Head Gardeners would have dismissed the man there and then, but not our Mr. Mills. He made the foreman take the damsons, then he escorted the man to his own home and made him give the fruit to his wife while he, the Head, looked on. This so shamed the man that he vowed he would never steal again.

It also made us in the bothy think carefully about the garden produce we were giving away to keep our own grub score low; it was something that apparently happened in most bothies, and our Head was most unlikely to be ignorant of that fact, so we excused ourselves for not feeling too guilty.

There was another occasion when our Head showed his nerve.

Each Friday Jim took Mr. Mills in the garden van to draw wages from the bank, a journey of about three miles. On this day they were passing a lorry when Peter the horse took fright and bolted. Jim tried to steady the animal, but Mr. Mills took over the reins and gave the horse his head for nearly two miles, then as Peter began to tire he got the whip and kept the horse at full gallop all the way to the bank. Peter was in a white sweat on arrival, but he had probably learnt a lesson; I never knew of him bolting again, though he was still temperamental at times, as I learnt to my cost.

Jim was away ill one week when I was on duty, so I had to feed and water the horse as part of my duty. I had been told not to touch Peter when going behind him in the stable, but this morning I was foolish enough to forget those instructions and I gave him a pat on the hindquarters. I promptly got a kick in the ribs, but fortunately for me the impact was taken by a metal cigarette case I had in my waistcoat pocket; it was flattened by the horse's hoof. I managed to get back to the bothy, but I was in considerable pain and, for the first time, I was unable to continue my duty.

Bert had to report the matter to Mr. Mills, who came to the bothy to see me. He was a bit concerned, and on the Monday morning a doctor was called in; he found I had two ribs cracked and one broken. A bothy is not a very suitable place for anyone who is ill, so our Head made arrangements for me to go home.

He found that the most convenient way for me to travel was by bus, as it ran on Tuesdays and passed quite near to my home. That two-and-a-quarter-hour journey was more than a little uncomfortable, but it was not without interest. As it passed through the villages the bus would pick up and set down passengers almost anywhere, and the driver, a certain Mr. Bell, and his conductor, Rupert, not only looked after their passengers but acted as parcel carriers. They would collect almost anything to take into town and would drop things off at any house the bus might pass. It was a service inherited from the horse-drawn carrier's cart which had for so long been the only means for people from the villages to travel to the nearest town to do shopping or to visit relations and friends.

Our Mr. Bell and Rupert were perhaps a bit special, because it was known they would always do some shopping for elderly or infirm people living in the villages. Everyone travelling in the bus seemed to know everyone else, so there was an air of friendliness all the way and the talking never stopped. The bus, on the other hand, stopped at every public house to set down or pick up passengers; the pub was the main stopping point in every village, and it was here that parcels, boxes, sometimes growing plants, would be collected or put on board.

When it was time for me to alight Mr. Bell, who knew of my injury, asked me where I lived. When I told him he said, "I'll drive you there, it'll only take a few minutes." In fact it took him several hundred yards off his route, but it appeared to be all part of the service, which was good value for one shilling and eightpence.

I was home for three weeks, and during that time I renewed my friendship with Dorothy, a girl I had known before I went to bothy. I spent a great deal of time with her and we got to know each other very well, so I was a little sorry when the time came for me to return to work.

Dorothy told me she had a cousin who lived in our village and I was able to tell her that we had met a few times in our "local". As I now had good reason to get to know him much better we became good friends. He was one of the very few self-employed people living in the district. He had a smallholding on which he grew vegetables for sale, and he also did repairs to farm machinery and was starting to do maintenance work on tractors as they became more and more common on the farms.

He was also the one man who owned a steam traction engine with a mobile thresher, elevator and sawbench. From early September Alf would go from farm to farm threshing the corn which had been put into ricks or into the barns. The flywheel on the traction engine powered the thresher and the elevator by means of belts. It was a busy scene in the stackyard as the sheaves of corn were fed into the threshing drum; the corn was discharged down chutes into bags while the straw was thrown out on to the elevator, being put into ricks to be used for bedding and for feeding to livestock during the winter.

During this operation many rats that had been feeding on the corn were disturbed, so the farmers would be in attendance with their men, guns and dogs to kill as many as possible. If it was known that there were many rats infesting the stacks the whole area would be enclosed in wire netting after the engine, thresher and elevator had been put into position ready to start work, thus ensuring that the pests could not get away. When work started the dogs and men with staves would make sure that every rat that reached the surrounding wire was destroyed, a gory business but very necessary.

Once all the harvest had been gathered in and safely stored away Alf would go into the woods with his engine and set up his sawbench, cutting timber for building purposes or else cutting logs to be sold for firewood.

When I had a chance I would go along to help with these activities, and in so doing I got to know most of the local farmers. I would often return to the bothy with something that would help keep our grub score down.

Unfortunately I could not go out with Alf as often as I would have wished. From September onwards I wanted to play football, but on many of our Saturdays we would have to go beating for the shooting parties.

Pheasant shooting was certainly the most popular of all the shoots, but wild duck provided a faster-moving target; duck shooting was reserved for those guests with the greatest skill. Our keepers usually raised about a thousand duck each year, and these were put on the lake when still quite young. They were fed to encourage them to stay where they could be found later, and of course quite a few of them did breed on the water's edge.

The lake was crossed by a road bridge at a point about half a mile from either end, so before the shooting season started hides were built on the bridge. For a time the birds would not fly over the bridge, but after a while they got used to the hides and no longer feared to fly over them.

On shooting days the guns and their loaders would take cover behind the hides while some of the beaters at one end of the lake started to make as much noise as possible, driving the duck up the lake and over the guns. The survivors usually landed at the other end of the lake, where there was another group of beaters to drive them back again.

It was noticeable that each time the birds flew over the bridge they would be flying higher than the time before. They would be driven back and forth for two to four hours, and by that time the game which did fly over the guns were much too high to kill, so that would be the end of the shoot for that day.

Much as I disliked all this killing of game birds, we in the bothy were not slow to find some dinners for ourselves. We would go out after the shoot to look for wounded birds which, of course, we were supposed to surrender to the keepers. We did give them to the keepers, but we first made sure we kept enough for two or three meals.

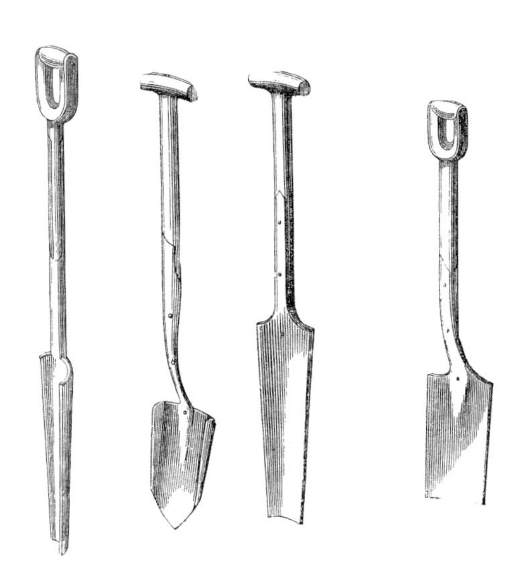

# A hard winter 7

WE HAD been troubled with rats living in a bank quite near our bothy, and the use of poison and gin-traps seemed to make little difference. Talking about it in the local one evening, Eli Dheon said he could easily get rid of them for us, so we invited him along to deal with these pests. Eli seemed highly pleased with the idea he had to rid us of our problem, but he would tell us nothing, and we were left wondering just what he was going to do.

He came along on a Sunday morning and asked us to cut a number of small turfs. Then, blocking up most of the holes with these turfs, he put calcium carbide in the rest and then blocked up the remaining holes after pouring water on the carbide. We thought he was just going to gas the vermin, but Eli had other ideas.

After a short time he removed the turf from four or five holes on the far side of the bank, then unblocked just one hole on the near side and put in a lighted taper. The resulting explosion was spectacular. The whole bank heaved, turf, stones and clods of earth were flung everywhere, and many rats came tumbling out, some dead, others dying.

Eli thought there might be more left inside, but digging soon showed us that there was nothing left alive. True enough, this was the end of our rat problem, but it had been too spectacular for our liking. It was fortunate that no one was hurt, and it taught us not to play around with carbide and water again.

Perhaps Eli was feeling a little guilty about this near-accident, because he invited us over to his house for a drink. Three of us were able to accept his invitation and cycled over later in the day.

The house was quite small for a family of five sons and three daughters. There were only four rooms, so sleeping would have been something of a problem but for the lovely caravan standing in the garden. That, we were told, was always kept in readiness to take to the road at any time that Joseph, the father, felt the need to move on.

The moment we went in we noticed how everything was so very clean and tidy. Mrs. Dheon made us welcome, offering us a mug of beer of her own making, and very good it was too. Then we had to see her rather lovely garden just as daylight was fading, and the scent was superb.

Having seen the garden, and smelt it, we went back inside to more beer and cake, while Dheon (as Joseph was known to his family) told us tales of gipsy life, and of their firm belief that they were a special people. It seemed to us that he took the opportunity to remind his family that they could only marry their own kith and kin. He went on to explain that he considered his family were subjects of the King, but they did not think of themselves as English but first and last as gipsies, and of this they had reason to be proud.

Gipsies were born to serve each other, he told us, and to work. That was why all of the children started to do some work from the age of four. Gipsies had to be tough, and clean, so the morning wash, outside and in all weathers, was essential. Every member must submit to the will of the head of the family, so ensuring harmony throughout the household. From what we had noticed during our short stay, Joseph was very much in command.

After a while it was suggested that we might like to hear their phonograph, and we were fascinated to see how this was set up. The machine was put near the edge of the table, then a kind of music stand like a big question mark was placed on the floor nearby to carry a large horn, which was attached to a speaker on the machine by a rubber tube. The motor was wound up and a cylinder, the shape of a cocoa tin but a bit larger, was pushed on to a revolving arm. Then the needle which was part of the vibrating disk speaker made contact with the now revolving black cylinder, and a scratchy yet reasonably clear music emerged. I think we were all more interested in this old machine than in the music we heard.

We enjoyed our evening with the Dheons, and could not fail to appreciate the marvellously happy atmosphere in the household.

As a parting present we were given two rabbits and a pheasant, all ready for cooking.

As the days got shorter our evening entertainments started up once more. The reading room, club nights and dances were our main attractions, along with the occasional evening in our local public house.

One cold night we went to a dance in the village hut, and late in the evening young Doug decided he would go for a drink. Unfortunately he drank more than was good for him, and then wandered off into the night. The landlord was a bit concerned and came over to tell us that he thought Doug had drunk too much and was far from well.

We gave the matter little thought, and went on dancing until midnight. We were fairly certain Doug could look after himself.

When we did return to the bothy there was no sign of Doug. Now it was our turn to be concerned, and the four of us went out to search for him. It was well past one o'clock when we found him asleep on a grass verge covered with frost. We had almost to carry him back to the bothy, and when we got him there we massaged his legs and arms and managed to get him to take a hot drink, then we put him to bed.

He was quite ill for several days, and the doctor said he had a severe chill and must stay in bed. Again the problem arose of illness in a bothy, but Doug could not be moved, so with the help of our bothy lady we did all we could to help him recover. No one ever spoke of his night on the grass, and the bothy code forbade us to inform the Head Gardener of the real reason he was off work. He made good progress, however, and was back at work before the busy Christmas period.

It was good to have him back at work, but I was also pleased he was better for another reason. I had a letter from my girl friend Dorothy telling me that she was going to spend two days of the Christmas holiday with her cousin Alf and his wife, and would I meet her at the railway station on Christmas Day evening at ten minutes to six. This I was only too pleased to do, of course.

The station was three miles from the bothy, and as it was

snowing a little I decided to walk rather than cycle. As I walked along the snow came down thicker, and by the time I arrived at the station it was about two inches deep. Alf drove to the station in his little two-seater car. The train was over an hour late, and by the time it came into the platform a blizzard was blowing. Dorothy had brought along her elder brother and sister, and we had a real problem as to how we could all get to the village. I thought it better if I walked back on my own and Alf took his guests in his car, but after thinking it over he decided I might well be useful if the snow was really bad on the country roads, so we agreed to go together.

We managed to get the two girls inside the car, while Dorothy's brother Jack and I packed ourselves in the open dicky seat at the back, which was meant for only one person. Alf put the luggage on our knees, and we set off through the blinding snow.

The road could be followed reasonably well for nearly a mile, even though we had to stop many times to clear the snow off the windscreen, but then the time came when it was impossible to go on as we were. Jack and I had to walk in front of the car to find the road for the driver, as we knew there were roadside ditches in places and these could no longer be seen. Several times we had to get the ladies out to help push the car through drifts, and for the last half-mile the little car was all but carried.

It was almost nine o'clock by the time we arrived in the village. It had taken us two hours to travel those three miles. We were all cold, wet and hungry, but after being given a hot drink and a meal we could see the funny side of our grim journey from the station. All the same, I was only too pleased to get back to the bothy for a few hours sleep.

We were all up early the next morning, for Bert realised that with the heavy fall of snow there would be much to do. Snow was still falling, but even so, our first task was to try to keep the pathways as clear as possible.

Though the use of the horse and van was out of the question, garden produce had to be taken to the mansion for the usual Boxing Day party, so the Head Gardener detailed the five of us, along with two men from the kitchen garden, to carry all that was needed in hampers. In places the going was difficult and we had to dig our way through some drifts, so we were late getting to the house and the Cook was really worried by the time we arrived. She had wanted the vegetables and fruit much earlier, as with guests and staff she had to cook for fifty-one people. We were given a lecture on getting up early in the morning, and the Cook alluded to the laziness of gardeners; it seemed that the weather outside should have made no difference to our timekeeping. We were assured that she would report us to our Head Gardener and to our employer if any of her meals were not on time.

Bert and I put on a new table centre, and we needed to make good several of our floral displays. We were very pleased to hear that the Boxing Day shoot had had to be called off, as that gave us hope that we might be able to finish early and have most of the day off. We had finished all we needed to do and were about to leave the "Big House" when the Butler sent for us. He wanted some toboggans brought down from an attic, scrubbed, and prepared for use by some of the house guests. We knew we dare not refuse, so we set about doing the job as quickly as possible.

When we had cleaned them they were inspected, and finding himself satisfied with our efforts the Butler called John, one of the footmen, gave him the key of the wine cellar, and told him to take us down to have a Christmas drink.

Perhaps it was a mistake to have let us into the cellar, because we stayed a long time sampling the various wines and beers. We were only too pleased to get back to the bothy in the afternoon to spend a few hours in bed, but Bert was the duty man and, the weather being so bad, he had to keep the greenhouse boilers going all day, and on into the night; there was no rest for him.

Next day we were all detailed to beat the many small trees and shrubs which were breaking down under the weight of the snow. Most of the soft fruits were grown inside a wire netting cage, and this had to be relieved of the heavy snow. What an unpleasant job that was; one had to go inside the cage to beat the snow from the top wire, and the snow fell down on to the beater below.

The roads leading up to the house and around the garden had to be cleared to give some sort of access, and so did the driveway to the village, and the paths around our bothy. Not having seen the postman or any of the usual roundsmen by lunchtime, and four of the garden staff having failed to appear for work, we came to realise that we were completely cut off from other villages.

Once we had got some semblance of communication on the estate, we met up with the farm hands to open up the roads out of the village. Everyone started digging with shovels, but after a while the Farm Bailiff sent a tractor on which had been fitted a home-made snowplough; this turned out to be a great success, and for the most part did all that was needed. It was then only the deepest drifts that needed a working party with shovels to break their way through.

This heavy snowfall brought some compensation for me, as Dorothy, her brother and sister were unable to return home as planned. I had the pleasure of her company for a further five evenings, by which time the roads had been cleared and the trains were running normally once more.

It remained very cold for the next two weeks, the temperatures at night falling to as low as thirty degrees of frost, and we had to be very careful with our thermometer readings because of the reports we made to the Met. Office. These low readings were checked by having three thermometers in the recording box. We were unable to give an accurate reading of the depth of snowfall because of the considerable drifting, but in sheltered places we measured fifteen inches.

The lake was frozen, but nobody was permitted to skate because of the wildfowl, and the keepers kept watch to see that no one disturbed their game. At least this time we were spared the chore of getting ice to go in the icehouse.

When the thaw came in mid-January it came all too quickly, causing considerable flooding. Some houses at the lower end of the village had water running into them, but as usual everyone was willing to help. Furniture, lino and in a few cases carpets were removed to the upstairs rooms until the water went down, then the men and women of the village got together to clean up those houses that had been inundated.

It was the attitude of the village people, always ready to help each other, that was greatly in evidence during this hard spell of weather, and it was to everyone's credit that no one really suffered hardship. The Dheon family took it upon themselves to look after the older people, supplying them with wood for fires with the help of Alf's traction engine and sawbench. As usual they kept the street taps thawed. The Women's Institute did great work for the old and for the children, who for the most part enjoyed the snow and ice.

It was the horses that suffered more than the people. The baker, the butcher and the oil man had to keep the people supplied, and their horses' shoes had to be roughed by the blacksmith to try to prevent them slipping. The roundsmen were careful to lead their animals all the time, but even so there were several occasions when horses fell and had to be helped to their feet by the drivers and anyone else who was at hand. Fortunately there were no reports of any of those marvellous animals being badly injured.

The cold, hard winter gradually and reluctantly gave way to spring, and the old adage "As the days lengthen, so the cold strengthens" was noticeably true. Even so, plant life will not wait, so we got busier day by day, which made it all the more surprising when Mr. Mills decided it was time for some changes in his staff.

Bill, the pleasure ground foreman, had been wanting to move for some time, and now he was found a situation as foreman, under glass, at Wollaton Hall, in Nottingham. He was delighted to get this post and could hardly wait to go to this important estate, but our Head would not be hurried. Bill had to wait two weeks before he could pack up his belongings and set out for Nottingham. We wished him well, and "Mum" cried a little, as usual when one of "her boys" left.

A new man, Reg Kayne, came to us from Townhill Park, in Hampshire, to take over from Bill as pleasure garden foreman, and I was moved from the glass houses to be first journeyman under Reg, who was about twenty-three. Young Doug was now made first journeyman in the job I had to vacate, so he too was very happy with these movements of labour. For my part, I knew I would get a lot of new experience, and working under a new man might be an added advantage.

Young Tom Tinchcombe was later engaged to make good the staff in the glass houses. He had come from a small estate in Sussex and this was his first job away from home, so he had to receive the usual lecture on bothy life. Like most people who came into bothy for the first time he was rather nervous for a few days.

Changes such as these were quite normal on the larger estates, and they usually worked to everyone's advantage. The Head could put his labour where it suited him, or he could bring in new staff by placing one or more of his men under other Head Gardeners in different parts of the country, so that we as workers gained new experience in other departments of our garden, or by being moved elsewhere. One of the disadvantages of working in these large gardens was the fact that the departments were rather watertight, so it was necessary for us to move from time to time to gather experience. If we were moved to another part of our garden it usually meant we were to stay for at least another year, but it was quite common practice for people to be moved on after two years.

I could now be fairly certain that my stay at Fonthill House would be for at least three years; I felt I had given Mr. Mills satisfactory service. One could never be quite sure just why Head Gardeners moved their men around as they did; we liked to think it was for our good, but we were often left wondering if this was really so. As for us, we were quite happy to do as we were told, knowing only too well the uncertain state of the labour market. Perhaps this was the reason men seldom asked for a move but awaited the pleasure of the Head.

Of course it was not long before the local girls knew there were fresh faces in the bothy, and once again rivalry between us and the village lads came to the surface for a while. Reg and Tom knew they had our support, should the need arise; fortunately nothing more than words were ever exchanged.

My transfer to the pleasure gardens meant I now had further to go to work, so Reg and I were always first away in the mornings. It also meant I no longer had breakfast in the bothy, but the Cook saw to it that we didn't do too badly most mornings and she would give us something to eat with our cup of tea. All the same, there was the odd occasion when it was inconvenient, and then we would have to go hungry until dinnertime.

We had to cross the bridge over the lake and walk up the drive to the mansion. Every morning nature would give us something new to observe, the ever-changing colour of the trees and fields, the activities of the birds and wild animals, the many runs made by rabbits, some very much worn by constant use. We discovered three favourite runs for foxes, and we saw these animals from time to time as well as the occasional stoat, and sometimes even weasels. Our gamekeepers were always ready to trap and shoot the foxes, stoats and weasels, as they lived almost entirely on rabbits, game birds and their eggs, but we found them fascinating to watch.

We were most intrigued when we noticed a pair of wild ducks building a nest high up in a cedar tree, about fifty yards from the lake. We thought this most unusual, as they generally made their nests on the lake or in the plant life growing on the water's edge. Each day as we passed on our way to and from work we watched progress, and at the end of the week we were sure the female was sitting on eggs. We were determined if we could to watch to see how the ducks would get their young down from the tree and into the water. We were very lucky indeed, as early one morning we saw the drake land on the water apparently with a duckling in its beak; he left the duckling with the mother, who already had two little ones with her. At first we could hardly believe what we had seen, but we kept out of sight and waited and watched. Soon the drake was away again, flying around for a short time, then he disappeared into the cedar tree and we lost sight of him for a while. After a short time he returned with another baby; this time it appeared the duckling was on its parent's back as the drake glided down. We watched as he did this twice more; the first young one fell into the water as the drake landed, but we were sure the second one was placed in the water, Dad using his bill to complete the operation. And there he remained on the water with his family of six.

We had to pass close to the cedar to get to our work, and there at the base of the tree we found five ducklings, four were dead and one nearly so. We were left wondering whether these ducklings had fallen from the nest as they tried to get on the drake's back, or had they died in the nest and been thrown out? To these questions we never found a satisfactory answer.

Mr. Mills was very interested to hear of our observations, and was pleased we had stayed to watch this act of nature. With his vast knowledge of the countryside and its wildlife he was well aware that some ducks did build their nests in trees, he understood that the young ducklings normally fell from the nest to the ground without sustaining much harm, but he had never seen this happen. He too was puzzled by the drake apparently carrying the young to water, and at the high mortality rate.

# Celebrations 8

MR. MORRISON'S son attained his majority in July and there were to be great celebrations. This, of course, meant a lot of work for us, and the preparations went on for some weeks. A large barn at the home farm was cleaned out and a new floor was put down for dancing, and we had to decorate the barn with flowering plants, cut flowers and ferns. We also decorated the marquee which was erected nearby and fitted out with tables.

Every employee on the estate, whether he worked for any of the tenant farmers or was employed directly by Mr. Morrison, was invited to a midday lunch. Nearly two hundred sat down to a five-course meal, followed by speeches and singing, and with plenty of wine and beer we were all quite merry and only too ready to sing.

After that enjoyable lunch Mr. Morrison laid on three motor cars to take back to their jobs anyone who had to return to work that afternoon, such as those involved in milking or feeding livestock. Of course, our duty man had much to do in the glasshouses, so two of us were detailed to help him.

Later on all the wives and families joined us for tea, which was followed by a social evening with dancing, housey-housey, or bingo as it is called now, and a whist drive. A concert party was engaged to keep the party going throughout the afternoon and evening and to keep the children amused when the adults were dancing to a six-man dance band. No one knew just how many people enjoyed the celebrations that evening, but it might well have been in excess of six hundred.

Mr. Morrison must have expected some people would drink more than was good for them, so he arranged for four motor cars to stand by to take home anyone who needed assistance. There were drinks on hand all the time, and we could have anything we asked for at the long bar. Nonetheless, priority was given to the women and children, who could order a car at any time to suit their needs. This was something few of the women had ever been able to do before, and for a few it was their first ever ride in a car.

It must have meant a great deal to Mr. Morrison to have his son John attain his twenty-first birthday, as no one had ever known such a party before, and none of the lads who had been in other bothies had ever seen or heard of such celebrations.

Three of us spent the next day removing our flowers and plants, these all being returned to the gardens. We were a little sad to see the lovely dance floor being taken up, as the barn had to be returned to its original use.

There was still a lot of beer left over, and what was not drunk was taken away by those of us who were doing the clearing up. The last dregs of the barrels were poured down the drain; the caterers made sure they took nothing back from any barrel or bottle which had been started.

One thing that to some extent spoilt the birthday party was the number of wasps around, so later in the week Mr. Mills told Reg and me to find all the nests around the garden and home farm and to destroy them. We were given cyanide for this purpose, and we had to be more than just careful using this dangerous gas. We were instructed to use gloves all the time, never to touch the small white knobs of cyanide with our hands, and never under any circumstances to put our hands near our nose or our mouth until we had had a thorough wash with soap under running water; we had to remember always that the gloves we used were heavily contaminated.

It was not too difficult to find the nests by watching the flight of the wasps, and of course we knew the kind of place wasps liked for their nests. Sometimes, though, it was not easy to get our cyanide to the most advantageous position; one needed to get some of the small pieces of cyanide into the nest, which was usually a few inches under the ground or in a bank. Usually we could place some pieces of cyanide in the nest by making use of the entrance made by the insects, then we poured water on the whole area to make it damp enough for the lumps to give off the deadly gas and made a quick retreat to a safe distance. Anyone nearby had to be warned to keep well away for at least half an hour. When it was safe for us to do so we would return to dig out the nest and destroy the many grubs that we found under the ground.

We had been supplied with protective clothing as well as bee-keepers' nets so that we could approach the nests in relative safety, and in this way we managed to account for over fifty colonies during that summer. One thing we did discover in the late summer was that a strong colony would often have an annexe in which only queen wasps were bred. In this annexe there might be well over a hundred queens or queen grubs, so in September these were our main target.

When we told our Head about our success, especially with the queens' nests, he was not particularly pleased. He told us that we had been far too ruthless in exterminating the wasps. He went on to explain that some wasps were needed in the natural order of things to keep the population of aphids within limits, and in turn to provide food for certain birds. This was something we had not even thought about; again we had to admire our Head's knowledge of the things that mattered in the countryside.

When the autumn leaves began to fall he explained to us that the covering of fallen leaves was Nature's way of protecting those trees which would otherwise be vulnerable to the winter weather, and at the same time of bringing to the surface plant food from deep in the ground in the form of those fallen leaves. He also tried to explain why it was a good thing to breed birds for shooting, but in that matter I was not convinced.

When Christmas came round it was noticeable that there were no guests arriving for the dinner and ball in horse-drawn carriages; the motor car was taking over at a considerable pace. Such changes were not for us, though; when we were out beating for the shoots we still had to walk everywhere and all day long, so we were pleased as the winter passed into spring that we had not been subjected to much bad weather.

Mr. Mills drew our attention to the low population of goldfinches, which do so much good in and around the garden, living as they do almost entirely on weed seeds. We were instructed to tell him of any pair that we saw building a nest. Only two pairs were seen, and they got special treatment. When the young birds were just hatched the nests were taken out of the trees and put into a box, with wire netting covering the open end. The holes in the netting were big enough to allow the goldfinches to get into the boxes, but too small for any predators to get at the baby birds. These boxes were then put back into the tree, water was supplied for the parents, together with some old carrot and lettuce seed. It was surprising how readily the birds got used to their nest and young being inside boxes.

When the youngsters were ready to fly the netting was removed, and in hours the young were on the wing. One pair made a second nest for a later brood, and again these were protected from harm, fed and watered under the watchful eye of our Head, so we knew that at least twelve young goldfinches were now in our area along with the four older ones.

Other birds, too, must have enjoyed that summer as we were bothered with swarms of flies which seemed to get everywhere. In the bothy we hung up a number of flypapers. Untold numbers of these pests died by sticking to these messy papers, which were changed every other week.

Each August there was a military tattoo at Tidworth, which was not all that far from us at Tisbury, and parties were made up to go by bus to see this spectacle. Sid Belmont, the local man with whom I had worked in the glasshouses, was very keen on a girl named Ann, who was very friendly with his sister Peggy. These two girls were never far apart, so Sid was making little progress with Ann, but the Tidworth Tattoo presented him with an opportunity. He asked me if I would make up a foursome with him and the two girls to go to see the tattoo.

I was to try to keep the two girls apart by taking on Peggy, and so leaving Sid clear to court Ann. To me it was something of a joke and I agreed to do as he asked.

The plan worked well, and Peggy and I spent almost all of that evening together. The tattoo was a really splendid sight, with massed bands of a thousand men marching and counter-marching to tremendous applause, the gun-carriage display by the Royal Horse Artillery timed to the second, and a mock tank battle which proved quite exciting, as were the exercises by gymnasts from the Royal Marines and the Navy. These men all put on a superb show, and under floodlights it was a most impressive spectacle.

We saw nothing of Sid and Ann until the time came for us to find our bus for the journey home. They told us they had seen very little of the tattoo, but they must have found they had so very much in common. In fact it seemed they had fallen for each other in a big way, as they were pleased to tell everyone on the bus that they intended to become engaged, if Ann's parents would give their consent. Peggy was delighted with this news, and I was pleased for Sid. He said he could never hope to be out of debt to me, but as Peggy and I had enjoyed each other's company there was little reason for him to thank me.

Things began to happen fast after that. In September all of us from the bothy were invited to the engagement party, where we were told that Sid and Ann would marry before Christmas, as Mr. Mills could promise them an estate house in December; they had to take it by the New Year or it would have to go to one of the farm hands.

Peggy and I were both pleased we had done something to bring Sid and Ann together. Perhaps that was the reason our friendship continued for a while, we were together at the wedding and now Peggy came along to most of the dances; it became almost a pleasure to teach her to dance.

She and I decided to join in with a group who were hiring a bus for the journey to my home town to see the talking pictures that everyone was talking about. Every seat in the bus was very quickly taken, and thirty-two villagers made the trip; more would have liked to have come along if there had been more seats. We had to leave early in the evening to make sure we arrived in time for the 8.45 house.

When we reached the Picture House there was a long queue, but everyone who had made the trip managed to get a seat. We didn't worry over much when we heard that the price of the entrance tickets had doubled to three shillings and sixpence.

The first film was the usual silent film we had all seen before. Expectations ran high during the interval as the little band of four who had played during the showing of the silent film left the orchestra pit; we realised we were in for an entirely new experience.

The lights dimmed, then the sound of music came from behind the screen. The curtains parted, the credits came on the screen, and the film "King of the Khyber Rifles" began. We were enthralled to hear the actors speaking and to see them doing so, it was something new to us to see and hear a door close, to hear the crack of a rifle shot, then to see and hear horses galloping. We even heard the sound of a key turning in a lock.

All this was new and exciting. At the end of the film everyone stood up and clapped, and nobody, it seemed, wanted to leave the cinema. Everyone just stood waiting, we didn't know what for, then at last the four musicians came back into the pit and played the National Anthem. That, of course, was the signal for everyone to make their way to the door.

The long journey back passed very quickly, with everyone talking about this new phenomenon and making plans for another visit to the talkies. For a few months it was something of a status symbol to have seen a talking picture.

It was shortly after this that the friendship between Peggy and me had to come to an end. I was called into the Head's office and told that I was to be moved to Norman Court, near Tytherly, between Salisbury and Romsey in Hampshire, as first journeyman in the plant and fruit houses under a new Head Gardener, Mr. Parsons.

Mr. Parsons had been in bothy with Mr. Mills some years earlier, and he was now in charge of a good garden, with a large staff, so Mr. Mills thought I would benefit by going there.

I was a little sad at first, as I had been very happy under Mr. Mills, and I respected him a great deal. I had also made a lot of friends, so I didn't really want to move from Fonthill House, but I had no choice in the matter. I knew it would be no use protesting, as the Head obviously had someone in mind to take my place. That was the system; I suppose it was to some extent feudal, yet we were really the lucky ones, having a home and a job when so many people had neither.

I had just a week to take leave of my many friends. Peggy was quite upset at my going, and I had to promise I would write to her, and would try to come back to see her again. Sid said he would be able to put me up at any time I cared to return; I think he wanted me to visit them often, as I knew he was very fond of his sister and didn't like to see her unhappy.

I too was sorry to leave Peggy, as she and I had become good friends. That's how I would have liked it to stay, but it was painfully clear that she wanted more than friendship, and I could not give her what she wanted. I had to make those promises to her, hoping that when I was away she would gradually lose interest in me.

"Mum" too had her little weep, as usual, so I promised her that I would let her know how I got on in my new job.

On the morning of the fourth of February I packed my case to await Jim, who was to drive me to the station after I had said farewell to my bothy mates. Once more I was to travel behind Peter, with Jim talking all the way to the station as usual, but my thoughts were very different during this ride from those I'd had on that first journey from the station. No longer was I pleased to ride behind a horse; I had got used to trains, buses and motor cars, and I felt I had grown up and matured over the years I had spent at Fonthill House and could now face anything that was before me.

I had to call to see Mr. Mills before leaving. He gave me the written references he had promised, which he knew would be a vital document for me to keep for my future. He told me that I was to keep in touch with him, and if at any time I needed help I was to write at once and he would be ready to give me any assistance he could.

For my part I thanked him for all the training he had given me, and for the guidance he had given me on living. Then, for the first time, he told me I had done a good job for him, and he would expect me to do the same for my new Head.

# An unpleasant change 9

THE journey to the small town of Romsey was rather tedious. When I changed trains at Salisbury I had time enough to study the advertisements on the station hoardings: it seemed you must read the *Daily Chronicle*, take Milo Tonic Food and then let Carter's Little Liver Pills keep you from all pain. Beecham's Pills were "worth a guinea a box," you should have joined the Mustard Club, washed in Wright's coal tar soap, done your fretwork with Hobbies, and, if you wanted to jump over a fence, then you should take enough Kruchens to cover a sixpence, but after reading all these advertisements I decided to go to the chocolate machine. I drew out two penny bars of Nestlés and a bar of Sharp's Creamy Toffee.

It was late afternoon before I arrived at my destination, to be met at the station by the garden horse and van. Jack Harris was the carter for Norman Court gardens, and the rather old van in which we drove to the gardens was drawn by Susan, a young, rather frisky, grey filly. We had only just started on our two-mile trip when Jack wanted to know why I had been foolish enough to come to Norman Court, asking didn't I know that no one stayed long with Mr. Parsons. I was somewhat taken aback at this, and wondered what I had let myself in for, but I remembered my mother's parting words when I had first left home.

By the time we arrived at the bothy it was dark, and it was in the dim light of two oil lamps that I made the acquaintance of my bothy companions. Jim was the plant and fruit house foreman, he had charge of the bothy, and I was to work under him, so it was he who bade me welcome. Cyril was second journeyman, so he would work under me, Harold worked in the kitchen garden under a local foreman, and Fred, the pleasure garden foreman, had Tim working with him.

Cyril was setting the table for tea, so I assumed he was the duty man that week. The meal was much as I had expected, the tablecloth was clean, though it had seen better days, and the tea was served in mugs, two of them enamel, the other four a thick ware. By the time the meal was finished I was already getting to know my new bothy mates, and they in turn were beginning to learn something of me.

I was now able to take stock of my new surroundings. One came through the outside door into the stone-floored washroom; the sink and wooden draining board was behind the entrance door. There was no water laid on, but several buckets stood nearby, some of them with water in. I was soon to discover that we each had our

**At Norman Court we each had our own bucket for washing, as shown here by Toni Goffe.**

own bucket, and this was the only means we had of washing, or for that matter bathing. There were a few cleaning utensils at the far end, but nothing more.

A door led from here into the living room, and this was very poorly furnished. Round the table, where I had my first meal, were four chairs and two stools which, with an old outdoor garden seat, were the only things to sit on. A small dresser on one wall had the usual crockery on the shelves, and across from the dresser was the black open-type cooking range, with just one oven and a hotplate.

Under the window at the far end was another small table with a shove-ha'penny board and a pile of *Gardeners' Chronicles*. The remaining wall was bare, with the entrance door at one end and the stairway door at the other. The floor was partly covered with plain brown lino, and a piece of coconut matting served as a hearthrug. Everything looked worn out and shoddy; obviously no one had any pride in this drab bothy, yet it was all reasonably clean.

There was another door near the kitchen range which led into what was called the sitting room. This was something of a joke, as there were no furnishings of any kind except for a pair of rather tatty curtains at the one small window. The room was being used as a boxroom: there was a pile of books on the bare floorboards, some clothes were hanging from hooks around the walls, and in a corner stood an old Valor oil heater which gave no appearance of ever being used. The same applied to the rather lovely, if old-fashioned, fireplace.

The stairs led up to a small landing with doors to the right and left. The one on the right led into the bedroom occupied by the two foremen, the one on the left led to a very small room with just enough space for a single bed. Small as this room was, it served as the only way into a third bedroom; the door into this third room was only three feet high, and had I not been shown the way I might never have discovered the room where I was to sleep in company with Harold and Tim. I learnt later that it was impossible to put in a door of normal height because a large beam went the full length of the wall carrying the weight of many roof timbers.

I was warned that I would bump my head at least once before I got used to the low doorway, and so it proved. In our room a large cupboard was built into one wall for use as a wardrobe, which we shared. There was very little space between our three beds, but at the foot of the beds, where stood a chest of drawers, we found just enough room to dress. Under the one window was a small table on which was an old swing mirror; it was a case of using the mirror in turn.

Having been shown which bed was to be mine, I turned down the bedding, but by the light of two candles there was little I could see. Tim assured me that all the covers were clean, though some of the mattresses were far from new. As I unpacked my case I was not too happy with what I had seen, but Tim and Harold seemed to be happy enough with things as they were, and if they could manage, so could I.

Some of the lads went out that evening, but Cyril and Jim stayed with me in the bothy. I was pleased about that, as I had a few things on my mind which needed answering. When I asked what Jack had meant when he said nobody stayed long in these gardens, Jim advised me not to take much notice of what Jack had said, but he did admit that this was a hard place to work. The Head Gardener was, he said, something of a driver, but Jim was careful to point out

**Candles lit us to bed—another sketch by Tom Goffe.**

the advantages of working at Norman Court—he was quite sure this was one of the best gardens in the South, and I would gain a lot of experience, growing a wide range of plants and fruit.

The floral work in the Court was on a grand scale when the family was in residence, Jim told me, and I would have a great opportunity to learn much about floral art. Every day we would have to pass through the kitchen garden on our way to and from the glasshouses, and he advised me to take note of everything that was being grown outside. At times I would have to work in with Tom, the kitchen garden foreman, who would be growing a lot of his early and late vegetables in some of the glasshouses I would have in my charge, and I would therefore be able to learn a great deal about growing vegetables under glass.

All this was very interesting, and I could see I would have a chance to widen my knowledge considerably. I was beginning to feel much happier about coming here to work when Jim started to tell me some of the difficulties of working under Mr. Parsons. When on duty, I was informed, we were not allowed outside the garden gate throughout the whole of the week, a rule that was very strictly adhered to. No one dared to be late starting work, yet at the other end of the day people were expected to carry on working if the job they were doing could be finished in a short time; the Head Gardener would decided what was meant by "a short time".

Cyril and Jim warned me that I could expect to see Mr. Parsons going around making sure that we had not left any dirt on the doors or handles as we went in and out. He would accept no slovenly habits, I was told, and expected his men to be always on their toes.

Jim also told me that the temperatures in all the greenhouses were carefully checked every night, both by the Head Gardener and by himself, and as usual those temperatures must be within two degrees of that set out on the greenhouse chart. So he hoped I understood boiler work, and could handle the four Robin Hood type boilers, those long, low sectional boilers that can have anything from four to nine sections. Fed from the front, the greater part of the fire is pushed towards the back as it burns so that great heat passed through the flues.

I was able to assure him that I did indeed understand boiler work, and was well used to the Robin Hood. Jim was pleased to hear this, but he went on to stress many times the need always to have the temperature as near right as possible.

Why were there not enough chairs for everyone to sit at table, I asked Jim, and why was the sitting room not furnished? Jim told me he had asked Mr. Parsons about putting in more furniture and had requested that water be brought inside, but it seemed the Head did not think it was good for men in a bothy to be too comfortable. He didn't want his men to get soft, and anyway, it would cost money that could be better spent on growing plants.

It might sound—and look—a bit rough, said Jim, but he advised me to stick it for a year or two, work hard, and gain all the experience I could in as short a time as possible. I would, he said, be wise to keep a civil tongue and not complain, as Mr. Parsons thought nothing of giving a man his cards and ordering him out at once. Remembering all those people who would have been only too pleased to have had my job, I resolved to make a go of the situation. I retired in a very thoughtful mood, only to find that I had a most uncomfortable bed to add to my troubles.

We were all up early in the morning, and at half past six we went out to start work. Mr. Parsons was outside the bothy to check that everyone was on time. When he saw me he told me to go to his office and wait there as he wanted to talk to me. When he had seen all the staff were in and on time, he came to the office and called me inside. I said "Good morning, Sir," but got no reply.

This was the first time I had really seen Mr. Parsons. He was a short, thin, almost small man with sharp features and small piercing eyes. One got the feeling that here was a man who could never relax. He looked at me for a while, then said sharply "Can you work?" and, without giving me time to reply, said "What use were you to Mr. Mills?" immediately followed by "Are you ever ill?" Without pausing for an answer he went on "You will always do as you are told, and quickly, make sure you are never late, and remember to wear a collar and tie at all times, I will not have my men coming to work half dressed." Before I could speak he added "Go on now, I'll soon see if you are any good to me."

Jim was waiting to show me what I had to do. I told him about my one-sided interview with Mr. Parsons, and was told that was quite usual for a new man. Never wish the Head "Good morning," he told me, we must wait for him to speak first—and I would find that Mr. Parsons never spoke to any of his men except to give an order, or if he wanted to know something about what we were doing. What was more, said Jim, I'd be well advised to stand still when the Head was speaking to me and look him straight in the face. That way the conversation would be short, if sharp at times, but I would not be subjected to a lot of questions.

First of all Jim took me into a range of glasshouses. We went through two peach houses, three vineries, four plant houses and a rose house, all of which were heated. Then he led me into a cold lean-to peach case with twelve peach and nectarine trees tied to wires on the back wall. There was a narrow footpath near the trees, and on the other side of the path were growing several hundred lettuce and cauliflower plants, which would mature where they were now growing. Then followed a patch of pansies in small pots, for planting outside later, and quite a number of Canterbury bells growing in seven-inch pots, to flower later.

At the far end of this long peach case we went down some steps into a heated underground forcing room for rhubarb, seakale, endive and chicory. It was dark in there; the only light was that admitted when you opened the door. The temperature in the forcing room was kept at fifty degrees, and Jim impressed on me the importance of keeping the door tightly closed so that the plants should grow in complete darkness.

All that I had seen so far was to be in my care. That was not the end of my tour, though, because Jim led me on through the whole garden. He was in charge of two cucumber houses, three melon and two carnation houses, and had a large stove house for tropical plants, built against a wall. In there was a hanging rockery for the smaller tropical plants. All the stonework was very like pumice so that the small plants could send their roots into the stones; this was particularly the case with some of the little orchids.

We then came to the glass which was allocated to Cyril. He had a fernery, another vinery, chrysanthemum and tomato houses, and a camellia house, which I could see would be his special pride. Some of those lovely plants were trained as fans, on canes and wire, others were bushes, or half-standards; all were in pots or tubs, obviously destined for the Court when in flower.

I was very interested in the large kitchen garden, which was divided into eight plots, each of them surrounded with espaliers, trained apple and pear trees. The borders between the trees and the pathways were used mainly for growing cut flowers which were needed in some quantity in the Court. The whole area of glass and kitchen garden was surrounded by a high wall. The bothy was built into the wall along the north side, then came lean-to sheds, one of the boiler houses, and a long fig house. Trained fruit trees were growing on the south and west-facing walls.

Part of the west wall was heated by a large open fireplace, built into the wall where it joined the north wall. A flue from this fireplace ran inside the wall for about forty feet, gradually rising, then turning back on itself and still rising to a point above the fireplace, where a chimney was provided to emit the smoke and at the same time draw the heat along the flue. When the trees on this part of the wall were in flower faggots of wood were burned in the open fireplace, and the heat passing along the flue was sufficient to keep the wall warm enough to protect the flowers during frosty nights.

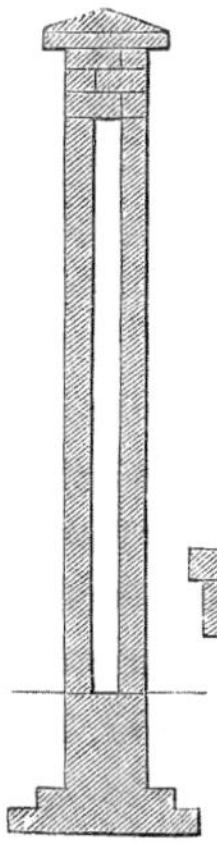

A second boiler house at the top end of the east wall had only a single boiler to heat the lean-to house on that wall. There was yet another wall running east to west, dividing the whole garden into two parts. Leaning against this was a second potting shed, the Head's office, two fruit rooms and two of the vineries. The one break in this middle wall was the Head Gardener's house and the garden clock tower. The only way into this walled-in garden was near the bothy, where a pair of elaborate wrought-iron gates under a stone and brick archway made a very impressive entrance. It was here that Mr. Parsons would stand, watch in hand, every morning at half past six to check the time of each man as he arrived for work.

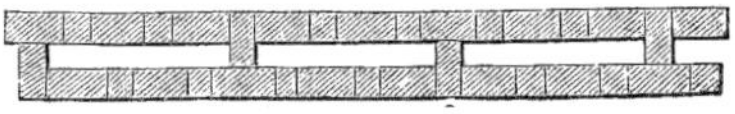

It was not good enough just to be in the garden on time, we had to be at our work. The glasshouses had to be unlocked, and opened if necessary; the men in the kitchen garden must get to their jobs with the tools they needed; and the pleasure ground people had to report before proceeding to the Court.

This whole procedure was repeated after the midday meal. In the evening the whole thing was in reverse, nobody could leave his job until the approved time, so the cleaning of tools and the closing down of houses had to be done in our own time.

Just outside the bothy was a water toilet for the use of all the garden staff, not just for those of us in the bothy. This was kept scrupulously clean by one of the garden boys. It was an offence even to leave the toilet roll partly unrolled on leaving; this was understandable, as to us it was something of a luxury even to be provided with toilet rolls.

There was a tap outside the toilet, and it was from here that we got our water for the bothy. I could see no reason why a pipe should not have been fitted from this supply to bring water into the bothy, but even this simple idea had been firmly turned down by our Head, so we continued to bring in our water in buckets and cans.

The irony of this was that water was laid on to the stable for the garden horse, and every glasshouse had its tap for the plants as well as soft water tanks, kept supplied with water from off the roof, in most of the houses.

Not only did we have to make do with water from buckets but this was not very helpful to the bothy lady. True, we made sure she had enough for her general needs, but cooking and drinking water was drawn from the outside tap as it was needed.

My new "Mum" was a middle-aged person called Mrs. Frost. She and her daughter shared the work in the bothy between them. They did their work well enough, but they did only what they needed to do—we all agreed this was partly because we were not in a position to supply "Mum" with any garden produce.

We often talked between ourselves about the way the many "Mums" around the country kept good larders from the gardens, and what they did for their "boys" in return, but at Norman Court there was no way we could help, so we had to do many of the little chores ourselves. Our Head knew only too well what happened in most bothies, and he was ever watchful to see that our Mrs. Frost did not go home with anything from the garden.

This was not a good estate on which to do much in the way of poaching as no game was bred there and no gamekeepers were employed. We hardly ever saw a pheasant or a partridge, which made me remember what my previous Head Gardener had said about shooting being necessary to keep up the stock of wild birds. I could see now that when keepers fed their game, other wild birds used to take some of the food. This aided the breeding of many wild birds, and in their turn even birds of prey derived some benefit from the action of the keepers.

There were plenty of rabbits, and we did manage to catch some of these, thus making some difference to our grub score which was in the region of twelve shillings a week. This did seem rather high, but it was offset to some extent as my wages were now twenty-seven shillings and sixpence a week, plus five shillings when on "duty".

There were four of us who did "duty", so every fourth week I found myself confined to the garden. Before starting our "duty" week we would need to stock up with cigarettes, or perhaps a bottle or two of beer. Beer was in screw-top bottles so it did not go flat if one drank only a part of the contents of the bottle, but this was not the case with lemonade; once you had pushed down the glass marble inside the neck of the bottle there was no way of resealing it. However, as we always kept a supply of Eiffel Tower lemonade powder this did not present too much of a problem.

"Duty" week started at half past six on Saturday morning. The first job was to unlock all the glasshouses, then when the heat was on one would need to attend to the boilers as quickly as possible. Cleaning and refuelling these boilers was the most important part of our "duty" during Autumn, Winter and Spring, while in the Spring and early Summer it was vital to keep a close watch on the opening and closing of greenhouse ventilators as the sun gathered or lost its strength.

Grapes are particularly vulnerable to sudden changes of temperature, so the vineries would need opening or closing perhaps as many as seven or eight times in a day. Peaches, too, can easily scald with a sudden burst of hot sunshine, and many plants in pots can soon show distress if the thermometer should rise or fall too quickly.

I was not really surprised to find myself on duty when Christmas arrived. This was often arranged between those men who did the "duties" when a new boy came into their bothy. That year Christmas Day fell on a Monday, so we were to have three and a half days' holiday, from two o'clock on the Saturday. Three of the lads were allowed to go home, provided they could be back in the bothy on Boxing Day. I was kept busy most of the time with my fires and greenhouses to attend to, while Harold and Tim were detailed to see to all the requirements at the Court over the holiday.

Our employer, W.M.G. Singer, Esq., and his family went abroad for the Christmas period, so the demands from the Court did not amount to very much. The servants had a party to which we were invited, but being on "duty" I could not attend. Tim and Harold did the honours for the bothy, and when they returned they brought with them some Christmas fare which the Cook had been pleased to let us have. So even if the three of us could not go away, we did have plenty to eat and drink for a couple of days.

Jim, Cyril and Fred all managed to get back on Boxing Day in time to go to a dance at the village hall, so it was the early hours of the morning when they came in. Somehow Mr. Parsons knew the lads were at this dance, so on the following day he was waiting outside the bothy door well before we were due to start work. It was a very dark and wet morning, but we knew he was standing there, and as we were a little late getting up we expected some trouble.

Jim, being foreman, decided that if some of us were going to be late, we would all be late and go out of the bothy together. Out we went in a group, and were each told by the Head to report to his office, there to await his pleasure; we didn't like the sound of that at all. When he arrived he had one of the pleasure ground men with him.

The seven of us were allowed to stand just inside the office, out of the rain, there to be reminded in no uncertain manner of our duty always to be at work on time. Jim thought it prudent to apologise on behalf of us all, but the Head seemed to take little notice, all we got was a further lecture, then we were dismissed. We thought that was the end of the matter, but it seemed that Mr. Parsons could

**Norman Court.**

neither forget nor forgive; when Tim went into the office to get his wages later in the week he was given a week's notice to leave.

It appeared that he had been warned before about being late, and had also been reprimanded about smoking during working hours. We were all very upset when we heard he had to go, but we knew there was very little we could do about it. Even so, we did decide we would try: Jim composed a letter, which we all signed, asking Mr. Parsons if he would reconsider his decision to send Tim away. The letter was posted that evening; we waited for some reaction, but nothing happened—our letter was completely ignored.

Tim worked out his week's notice, then packed his belongings. We hoped Jack would take him to the station in the van, but he had no orders to do so and dared not take the horse without permission. Two of us took Tim's two cases to the station on our bikes during our dinner hour.

Tim was pleased with the efforts we had made for him, but he wasn't sorry to leave the garden, even though he had no work to go to.

# The Chelsea Flower Show 10

IT WAS two weeks later that George Titt arrived to take over the journeyman's job in the pleasure gardens. He had come from Longford Castle at Britford, not very far from Salisbury, one of the leading establishments in that part of the country.

Of course, we accepted him without prejudice, as Tim's sacking was no fault of his. Coming from another bothy, he was made welcome as a person and as someone who would be able to give us more information on other gardens around the country, something we were always in search of.

Mr. Parsons now decided to make other changes. He engaged a local lad to help in the glasshouses so that I could be relieved of some of my growing duties in order that I could take over at the Court as flower decorator, and so that Jim would be able to spend more time growing. I was very pleased with these arrangements, as it meant that I would be able to see the pleasure grounds around the Court in some detail. I would also be doing a job in which I was very interested and at the same time would be able to leave the walled garden, even when on "duty," as the Court was a little over half a mile from the bothy.

Each morning I would cycle that half-mile along an avenue of rather lovely old lime trees which gave way to a short avenue of Irish yews before opening out into a large square forecourt. On two sides there was a low wall with a balustrade built on top; growing there were various climbing and rambling roses, interplanted with clematis and vines.

The mansion was a large, rather modern building with more than fifty rooms, including the servants' quarters. The front door that faced on to the forecourt was in fact two sets of double doors, one set opening outwards and the other inwards; all four doors were carved oak, and very imposing.

To the south was an extensive unbroken lawn in two areas,

surrounded on three sides by wide borders. Some of these were bedded out with spring and summer flowering plants; there were many roses in groups of about two hundred, also acres planted with herbaceous plants and several groups of flowering shrubs. Beyond the gardens on the south and west sides was open parkland, used as grazing for sheep and cattle. There were no fences between the park and the garden, as the whole of the garden was surrounded by a haw-haw, a ditch about eight feet wide and five or six feet deep with a gentle slope on the park side and a wall built up to ground level on the garden side. Looking from the mansion one saw only an unbroken landscape, with the garden merging into the park, yet the animals inhabiting the parkland could walk into the ditch but no further; the hidden wall was an unclimbable obstacle, and they could only return to their pasture up the slope.

Why this type of protection is called a haw-haw is still something of a mystery. It has various spellings in different parts of the country, and seems to be a very English idea; perhaps it was something introduced by Capability Brown.

On the east side of the mansion was a large winter garden, sometimes called a conservatory. This iron-framed house rose in the middle to seventy feet to give space for the several varieties of palm that we grew there; some almost reached to the glass roof. These palms were grown in large square tubs which had handles and were surrounded by brass bands. Under the palms and around the sides of the conservatory we grew many tropical flowering plants, changed regularly with new stock from the growing houses.

Acting as an annexe to the winter garden was an orangery, a large glasshouse with ornate stone pillars supporting the roof. These pillars provided an opportunity to grow a number of climbing plants inside the orangery. The floor was paved with white and black tiles, and on them stood fifty or so wooden tubs containing orange and lemon trees. These are interesting plants as they come into flower while they still bear ripe fruits from the previous season, and the scent from the white flowers was at times overpowering.

During the four summer months all the citrus trees were taken into the mansion forecourt near the main entrance and placed to form an avenue leading to the carved oak doors.

Going out of the east door of the winter garden one came to an extensive rock garden, built around a natural spring. Following the little stream that issued from the spring one came to a wild garden where the lovely specimen trees captured the attention. The trees were underplanted with heathers, rhododendrons and many other shrubs, together with countless daffodils and snowdrops. The little stream meandered through the woodland to a point where it was carried over the haw-haw in a metal canal large enough to take the water when the stream was in full spate.

With my new duties I found myself spending a lot of my time at the Court, decorating in the house and working in the winter garden. In the main rooms only cut flowers were used; these would be in large vases or bowls, giving an opportunity to make bold displays, always taking care not to have bright colours in a room where there were pastel shades and at the same time making certain my efforts blended or contrasted with the decor of the room.

Some of this was new to me, and I depended on Jim quite a lot during my early days as decorator; he taught me a great deal. His words were coming true, this really was a good garden in which to learn one's profession, even if life was a little difficult at times.

One evening during my week "on the wheel" it was necessary for me to put a new centrepiece on the dining table, and instead of returning to the bothy by way of the lime avenue I made a detour into the village to buy some cigarettes. I suppose I must have been seen going into or leaving the shop, because the next morning I was summoned to the Head's office. I received a severe warning that I must return directly from the Court to the bothy when on "duty" and not by way of the village. Failure to carry out this order, I was told sternly, might well mean dismissal; at the very least I would have my decorating job taken from me. I was also reminded that I still had to do some growing, and if I lost time doing my floral work at the Court it was up to me to make good by working in the evening.

As it happened, it did become necessary for those of us working in the glasshouses to do some work in our own time, and of course without thought of extra payment. There are certain jobs that cannot be done in the daytime, or which must be done in the shortest possible time. We were growing over a thousand chrysanthemums, and half that number of carnations, so when it came around to potting those plants it was important to get them done as soon as possible. Now this kind of work is very time-consuming, and as we were expected to pot three hundred plants into seven-inch or even ten-inch pots each day this was a task we could not do in a normal working day.

Grape thinning is a job that can only be done in the evenings, as the sun can be blinding at times, unless one got a dull day when this thinning could be undertaken. We were producing several hundred bunches of grapes, and as each of these bunches might take as long as twenty minutes to thin, we were spending a lot of our own time in the vineries. Fumigating the greenhouses against pests or disease is another job that can only be done when the sun has lost its strength, so we had no choice but to work many hours after tea on that.

When we were working in the gardens after hours we saw a complete change in our Head. He would talk to us and be almost friendly; the subject of conversation would be gardening, and we realised all the more from such discussions how accomplished he was in his profession. He had learnt his gardening in some of the best gardens of the day and must have studied his subjects deeply, as some of the theories he expounded were very new and up-to-date. It became almost a pleasure to work late into the evening and to hear him talking in depth on gardening. We often wondered why he needed to be so morose during working hours, and why he should be so ruthless with the men.

There were four of us who did this work after normal hours, and we were more than a little surprised one day in early May when we were called into the office and told we were to be sent to the Chelsea Flower Show for a day, with our expenses paid. None of us had ever been to the show, but we were well aware that it was the highlight of the gardening calendar, so excitement ran high—except for George and Harold, who were not so lucky. For the four of us who were making the trip it was a treat we had never expected, and for me it was the first time I had had a day away from work, except for my one illness.

We could hardly wait for the day to come, it all seemed almost unbelievable to us. But come it did, and we made our way to the station, where we were met by Mr. Parsons, who had driven down in the garden van. He bought our third-class return tickets to London, but travelled first class himself.

The train journey was uneventful. For most of the way we were travelling through countryside, but as we neared our destination we looked out of the carriage window at houses packed tightly together, with little or no space for gardens; every inch of land seemed to be built on. These small, dingy terrace houses were mixed up with the many factories, all of them very dirty and forbidding; we agreed we would not like to live in such cramped conditions.

As we neared Waterloo our line seemed to merge into a great many tracks, with trains going into and out of London all puffing their dirty smoke over everything. When we arrived at the terminus I was surprised at the vastness of the station, but there was no time to stand and stare, we had to get on to the underground train, which itself was a new experience for me. Everybody seemed to be in a hurry, and one hardly managed to get inside when the doors shut and the train started off, roaring through the endless tunnel. It was just as well Mr. Parsons was with us or we might have got lost, but he guided us off the train at Sloane Square and we set off to walk to the Royal Hospital grounds.

What an experience! I was amazed at the magnificence and vastness of the show; it left a lasting impression on us all. The arrangements of cut flowers, the pot and bedding plants, the rock gardens and hardy plant exhibits, they all gave me much food for thought. I was surprised at the number of firms showing sundries, and began to realise that machines of many kinds were being shown for everything from hedge cutting to digging and spraying.

The time was coming when I would need to know how to use these new machines, and here was an opportunity to see them at work.

We spent a great deal of time in the huge marquee in which the larger seed firms had put up magnificent displays of flowers, flowering plants and bedding plants. It was, we gathered, the biggest tent ever erected. Some of the exhibits towered many feet into the air; some were sunk into the ground, where the use of water gave aquatic plants the appearance of being in their natural home.

Then there were large exhibits of vegetables, which to our surprise were just as colourful as the flowers. It was difficult at times to get near these showpieces, so many people were feasting their eyes on the beauty of it all, in spite of some of the stands being over two hundred feet around. There were also many smaller exhibits, everything from orchids to strawberries and from fruit trees to tiny rock plants, and every one just about perfect.

It was obvious that the people who grew these plants and staged these exhibits were specialists in getting nature to produce almost to perfection. I made up my mind there and then that I would become one of these specialists who could work with nature to the advantage of man, and of the plants.

We were still in the science department when the time came to meet Mr. Parsons at the memorial in the hospital grounds, first to have something to eat and then to start our journey home. On the train we had a chance to sit and consider all that we had seen at Chelsea. One thing had become very clear to us, that the standard of growing at Norman Court was in fact very high, and we could have done ourselves credit if we had been showing at this, the premier show in the country.

For the next few days the Chelsea Flower Show was the topic of conversation in the bothy. It was not too long, however, before we reverted to our usual line of table talk, about the jobs we were doing in our various departments from day to day. Of course, we all had our grumbles—very often about our Head.

A great deal of our talk was about the gardens and the bothies where the lads had worked before coming to Norman Court. We each learnt from the others many details about estates which might have good gardens in which to work, if the opportunity came along, and about the places to avoid. We were certainly agreed that when we left Norman Court none of us would recommend it to other men, not while Mr. Parsons was in charge.

We obtained a lot of information about other estates from the travellers for various seed and horticultural sundries firms, who were able to tell us a great deal about happenings in the garden world. They could often tell us where our ex-bothy friends were working and how they were progressing in our chosen profession. I was beginning to know quite a lot about such establishments as Blenheim Palace, Petworth House, Floors Castle and Chatsworth, and my hope was that one day I would be able to obtain a situation in at least one of these renowned gardens.

Some of these firms kept a register of employment, and their representatives were most helpful in letting us know where a situation might become vacant. They would also tell us where not to apply, should a post be advertised.

There were always a few positions advertised as vacant in our weekly magazine, *The Gardener's Chronicle*, but at the same time there might well be two pages given over to men looking for work, so we in the bothy always had a good idea of what was going on in the labour market. Although the balance was not at all encouraging we were all keeping a close watch on things, as none of us felt very secure. At times I wondered how much longer I could go on working under our Head and living in this most uncomfortable bothy.

And then, quite suddenly, there came a big change for the better.

# An unexpected visit 11

ONE DAY Mr. Singer came into the garden and must have decided he would look inside the bothy, something he had never been known to do before. We were having our midday meal when he walked in unannounced.

We all stood up as a mark of respect, but he told us to continue our meal. He looked around for a time, saying nothing, but it was plain to see he was far from pleased with what he saw. Then he asked how many of us were living in the bothy.

On being told that there were six of us, he inquired how six people could sit down to a meal with only four chairs. Jim mumbled something about managing, but we really didn't know quite what to say; we were still somewhat taken aback by this sudden visit.

Next thing, he wanted to see our sitting room. When he saw that it was empty he looked amazed, and very annoyed. On being told that we had no facilities for sitting he wanted to know why he had not been told of the conditions in which we were living. Then he wanted to know if our meals were satisfactory; we were able to assure him that we ate very well, as we did our own catering.

He then asked Jim to show him upstairs. There he made a careful inspection of the beds. He satisfied himself that they were clean, but he could see that they were in need of new mattresses, and he was far from pleased with the way we had to keep our clothes.

When he returned to the living room he wanted paper and pencil, and told us we were to sit still and be quiet. After a time he told us he was most displeased with us for having kept him in ignorance of the conditions inside the bothy, but he assured us that things would change, and quickly.

He was still very angry when he left to find Mr. Parsons. Although we were glad about this visit, we could not help wondering what the repercussions would be when our Head had his interview with our employer.

Two days later there were six upright wooden chairs around our table. They had been sent down from the Court; they might not have been new, but they were very welcome. It was nearly two weeks later that our sitting room was furnished, for the first time. We were given six new Windsor armchairs, a table, a bookcase and a brass table lamp. All our beds had new hair mattresses and two extra blankets, mirrors were bought for each bedroom, and three wardrobes were installed, which made our bedroom somewhat more cramped, but we were in no mood to grumble about that.

In addition to all that, water was now brought into the bothy by means of a hosepipe, just as a temporary measure. Then the sink had to be connected to the drains, which left us with six buckets we no longer needed. Never mind that, we were now more comfortable and the urge to leave was to some extent lessened.

Another thing that helped me to settle down that summer was being able to play cricket on Saturdays when not on "duty". I had joined up with a nearby village club and was able to establish a place for myself in most of the games. Our ground was not very good, only the playing square was mown and all the outfield was left for grazing sheep, so we played many of our matches away from home. Three of the away games were in Bournemouth, so on those days we were able to spend an hour or two by the sea.

I was feeling somewhat happier in the bothy, as I think we all were. On the other hand, our Head was not at all pleased about having to make so many changes in the bothy and became very sullen and difficult to please. Even when any of us were working in our own time he would no longer come near us or speak to us. We all knew we had to be very careful in what we said or did as he was obviously looking for any reason to get rid of us. For some weeks he was probing to find out who had invited our employer into the bothy; I think I might well have been his chief suspect, as he knew I did have occasion to see the owner and to speak to him and to members of his family when I was at the Court doing my floral work.

Towards the end of the summer the tension between us and Mr. Parsons began to fade, but even so we all continued to be very careful not to cross our Head, as we felt he had not forgotten. The harshness went from his manner as autumn turned to winter, but it was Christmas time before things really settled down and we could dismiss the matter from our minds.

I was not "on the wheel" over Christmas, so I took the opportunity to spend two days at home. My father thought the experience I was getting would serve me in good stead, but both my mother and my girl friend Dorothy seemed rather unhappy on my account. I had to assure them that I could manage to cope with the situation as it was.

In February Jack Harris fell ill, and as he lived on his own the doctor sent him to hospital. When we heard that Jack was very ill indeed Jim and I decided to visit him. He seemed pleased to see us, but said he was going to die, he had lived his "thousand moons" and was ready to go. We were not too sure what he meant by that, but on thinking it over we concluded that he must have meant he was well over seventy-six years old. That seemed incredible, as no one thought him to be much over sixty.

We were sorry to have to leave him, as we could not be sure we would see him again. Fred and Cyril went to see him the next weekend, and they were the last visitors he had.

We asked Mr. Parsons if we could send a wreath and were told we could buy whatever we liked, but he was not going to supply flowers from his garden. I don't think anyone ever forgave Mr. Parsons for that. A younger brother turned up at the funeral, and it transpired he was the only relative poor old Jack had. Jim was the only person permitted to represent the staff at the graveside.

Another Jack took over as the garden carter. He was Jack Mooning, who lived with his mother in the village.

Mr. Parsons went to the Chelsea Show as usual, but this time he made it quite obvious that nobody from the bothy was going to be invited along. The lads were disappointed, but it was not unexpected; we had to be satisfied with having a day without the Head around.

The summer passed without great incident, and I was reasonably happy in my work. Not only was I learning my own job but I was getting a good insight into the kitchen garden and pleasure garden work. Fred, the pleasure garden foreman, was a great help to us all, he was always pleased to share his knowledge with us and to keep us well informed of any new project that was taking place.

So it was with some regret as well as much pleasure that we heard that he was going to get married. We all knew he was courting Mabel, one of the housemaids at the Court; we had ribbed him many times about it. Whatever our pleasure at the news, it was soon discovered that Fred's marriage presented him and Mabel with some problems.

Fred knew he would have to leave the bothy, so he told Mr. Parsons of his intentions and asked if it would be possible for him to stay in his job and live in one of the many tied houses on the estate. Mr. Parsons said he expected he would be able to get a house for them somewhere on the estate—that would be a matter for the estate agent to decide—but he made it plain that Fred could not expect to keep his position as foreman in the pleasure garden as the man in that position must live in the bothy, so as to be available at any time.

It was later arranged that Fred should take charge of the rock garden, but he would be under the supervision of any new pleasure ground foreman. As he would no longer be a foreman his wages would be reduced by two shillings a week, and he would have to pay three shillings each week as rent when they moved into a house.

We felt it was hard and unfair that a man should have his money reduced by five shillings a week on getting married, at the very time when he would need more, as Mabel would have to give up her job on marrying. But Fred had little choice, he just had to accept what was on offer as he and Mabel had planned their wedding in September.

We knew he would move to another estate when an opportunity arose, so each of us decided to do what we could to help find him another post by getting into contact with Head Gardeners under whom we had previously worked. Fred registered himself with three seed firms who kept registers of employment as being in need of a situation as foreman in a good garden or as a Head on a smaller estate. He knew he dared not advertise in *The Gardener's Chronicle*; that would be seen by our Head, and Fred would risk getting the sack.

As things turned out we were all to miss the wedding. Jim received a letter from one of his previous Heads offering Fred a married foreman's position on an estate in Suffolk, if he could take up the post almost immediately. Fred was delighted to give in his notice, but Mr. Parsons was very cross, having already obtained a house on the estate for him. Fred was told to be out of the bothy by the end of the week, which made things a little difficult for him and his bride-to-be.

Fred had to be away on the Saturday, but Mabel was still at the Court, so it was arranged that he would go to Mabel's home in Bedfordshire and that she would follow him there to make the arrangements for their new home near Woodbridge. They would marry as soon as convenient in the small town of Sandy, which was much too far away for any of us to attend the wedding.

Some weeks passed before Bill Evans came to us from Belvoir Castle in Leicestershire, where he had been employed as first journeyman under glass for the Duke of Rutland. He was well used to bothy life, having worked in other important gardens, including Lord Derby's estate at Knowsley and the gardens at Panshanger in Hertfordshire, so it took him no time at all to settle down with us.

We were all very interested to hear about these important gardens, and he for his part was ever ready to tell us all we wanted to know. Although he was not yet twenty-two, he was a man of considerable experience. Bill was a very interesting person when he was talking about gardening, but his main topic of conversation was religion, a totally new talking point in the bothy. He knew his Bible very well, he read it daily and would often quote the Scriptures to us. Sometimes he did so to show us the folly of our ways, but always in a manner which gave no offence. He tried to assure us that what we thought of as our tribulations were in fact quite trivial and only sent to test us in preparation for the glorious times which we could inherit.

He really was a very persuasive fellow, and succeeded in getting us to go to church for Harvest Festival. This turned out to be very embarrassing for us as the Vicar, seeing us there for the first time, brought into his sermon a condemnation of those people who came to church but once a year, and then chose to mention in particular those men from a nearby bothy. This, we felt, was more than a little unfair as we could hardly answer back; no one from the Church had ever taken the trouble to call and see us, so this was our first and last attendance. Even Bill was annoyed at what had been said, but this did not deter him from trying very hard to make us change our ways, to give up smoking and to stay away from the local public house.

When the hunting season arrived I was kept very busy decorating at the Court. Our employer was Master of the hunt, and most weekends he would give a house party for as many as thirty staying guests. Every one of the guests had flowers and plants in their bedroom, and with masses of flowers used in the main rooms and the dining table having to be changed daily, I had very little time to do any growing, and even less time for myself at weekends, so I was ever grateful for the help I received from my compatriots in the bothy.

Mr. Singer employed three grooms to attend to his six hunters and two coach horses. The stables, almost half a mile from the Court, contained eight loose boxes for guests' horses, with a further eight for his own animals. The walls inside these boxes were tiled from floor to ceiling, the partitions were of oak, with sliding wrought-iron gates as an entrance to each box, and the floors were of small yellow bricks sloping down gently to drains just outside each box and inside the long wide corridor which ran the whole length of the stabling, forming two sides of a square.

There were three harness rooms, a saddle room, and two double coach houses, one of them used as a garage for two motor-cars. In the other was kept an old landau which Mr. Singer and his lady still used on fine Sundays to go to church for morning service. The whole stable complex, surrounding a large, square yard, was built of red brick and grey sandstone. The entrance to the yard was through a wide archway over which was the stable clock, with a bell loft above. The hourly striking of this bell could be heard over a major part of the estate, so the head groom had to make sure that it was kept accurately to time since it was regarded as the official time on our estate.

The training ground and grazing paddocks for the horses ran the whole length of the lime avenue down to the bothy, which was fortunate for us as mushrooms grew in abundance there in season. The kitchen garden staff would go out each morning gathering these delicacies for use by the Cook; then we and other workers on the estate were allowed to pick as many mushrooms as we needed for ourselves. We were not allowed to gather them for anybody but ourselves, not even for "Mum"; she would have to get her own, if she wanted any. At least, that was the rule, but of course we found a way around that little bit of nonsense.

The gathering of these mushrooms helped to keep our grub score at a reasonable level for a few weeks in the late summer. It was noticeable, however, that our food bill had gone up by something over a shilling in just one year. Not that we worried overmuch about that, as we still had money enough to buy most of the things we wanted.

We went to quite a few dances, and spent the occasional evening in the local pub, much to Bill's disapproval, and still we usually had something left over by the following pay day. Most of the bothy lads had money banked with the post office, on which we got two and a half per cent. interest.

It was just as well some of us were a little prudent, because although we didn't know it at the time we were in for a rude awakening. There had been much talk in the papers about the Wall Street money troubles, but all that was in America, a long way away, so far away that we never thought it was of any particular interest to us. In that we were wrong, so very wrong.

A few weeks before Christmas Mr. Singer announced that there would have to be a reduction of twenty men in the estate staff, and three of these were to be gardeners. Besides that, all wages would be cut by three shillings a week forthwith, throughout the whole of the staff. We were told there were money problems at the Court.

It seemed the first people to suffer were the members of the work force; the weekend parties in the mansion went on as before. Mr. Parsons decided that his best plan would be to dismiss the first journeyman from each of his departments, and as things were two of these would be from the bothy. So it was that George Titt from the pleasure garden and myself from the glasshouses were given one month's notice to find another situation.

Our Head told us he would do all he could to find us another job. He even said he was sorry to lose us, but as we were single men we were the ones best able to move. It did seem a pity that having so recently furnished the bothy for six men, it was now to be reduced to four.

We wrote to three seed firms asking them to put us on their register as being in need of employment. I put an advertisement in *The Gardener's Chronicle* for three weeks, then wrote to my previous Head Gardener, Mr. Mills, and informed my parents of our dismissal. Our bothy pals, too, wrote to their late Head Gardeners, so we had just a little hope that we might soon find another job.

We worked out our month, and at the end of it neither of us had received even an offer of an interview. I was able to go back home, but George had no home to go to and when we parted company he still did not know where he was going. I tried to persuade him to come home with me, but he would have none of that. To him that would have been charity, and he said he had had enough of charity in his time and would accept no more.

It was then that we realised we knew nothing of his background, and it seemed he was not going to tell us of it now. Perhaps he had no parents, but we never did know.

When I arrived home I was greeted by my girl friend Dorothy as well as by my parents. Father was somewhat concerned as to my future, but it was not long before he wanted to know about my progress as a gardener. His questions went on for some time, and my poor mother could hardly get a word in until Dad was satisfied that I was really learning my job.

Only then did he tell me that the letter Mother had been holding all the time was for me, from Mr. Denning, Head Gardener to Sir Felix Schuster and his daughter at Verdley Place, Fernhurst, a few miles south of Haslemere in Surrey. He asked for details of my experience. I decided that I must go to see him at my own expense, so I sent a telegram to say that I was coming.

Next morning I was on a train to Haslemere before eight o'clock. When I got there I had not the slightest idea where Verdley Place was, so for the first time in my life I hired a taxi. The drive took nearly a quarter of an hour, and the fare was seven shillings and fourpence. How very grateful I was for the pound note my parents had thrust upon me.

The interview with Mr. Denning lasted nearly half an hour. I could sense that I was making an impression; how pleased and relieved I was when he engaged me to start work the following Monday. However pleasing that decision was to me, it must have been a big disappointment to quite a number of men who had applied for the post, some of whom, like me, had come for an interview at their own expense.

When I got home that evening there was great joy in the house that I was not to join the unemployed. Even Dorothy was pleased about the job, though we knew we would have to part once again; we were at least able to enjoy one whole week in each other's company.

# Summary promotion 12

THOSE few days were very enjoyable, and in a way important to both of us, as Dorothy and I began to realise that we meant a great deal to each other. When I bade her goodbye on the Sunday evening it was with some sadness at parting, but also with joy in the fact that I was about to progress further towards my goal of becoming a Head Gardener.

The morning train was rather crowded and nobody seemed to want to speak, so I was not sorry when I arrived at Woking station, where I was met by the garden driver and taken to the bothy, this time by motor-van. Times were certainly changing: not only was the garden carter giving way to a driver, but in this motoring age things were moving faster.

It was early afternoon when we arrived at the bothy, so when I was left there on my own I had an opportunity of looking around. Once more I took stock of my new surroundings.

The bothy was above a potting shed and the fruit room. The outside stairway led up to a landing which was under an overhanging roof, but otherwise open to the elements. Three rooms led off this landing, the first one being the living room and kitchen; then came the two bedrooms.

The living room was rather small, just about eleven feet square, and a table, chairs and a dresser almost filled the room, leaving very little space for moving around. The sink, which with the draining board was in one corner, did at least have running water laid on. I noticed, too, that this bothy had electric light. An open-fire black kitchen range with an oven was fortunately built into a chimney breast and therefore took up none of the floor space, which was covered with the usual brown lino.

A fire was burning in the range, giving a comfortable atmosphere, and as everything looked clean and tidy I was feeling quite happy with what I had seen so far. I went out on to the landing again and entered the first bedroom, in which I saw two beds, a chest of drawers with a swing mirror, and a wardrobe. The bedlinen was clean and fresh, as were the two towels hanging on an old towel horse. Again, though, the room was small and rather dark, as there was only one small window looking out on to the garden wall.

The second bedroom was similar, but the outlook from this room was much better, for it overlooked the stable yard. As in the first bedroom there were two beds, a wardrobe, a chest, and again two towels, so I assumed there were four of us in the bothy.

I went down the stairs and across into the stable yard, where I found the water toilet. I ambled around for a time, but, having seen nobody, I thought it wise to go into the garden to report my arrival. Making my way towards the "Big House" I came upon one of the gardeners, who told me where I could find Mr. Denning.

I found him without difficulty. He was a short, rather fat man, and seemed a pleasant kind of person. He welcomed me to Verdley Place, and said he hoped I would settle down in the bothy with my three compatriots. To tell the truth, this made quite an impression on me, as it seemed a long time since I had had a kindly word from my Head.

He explained my duties to me in considerable detail. I was to have charge of all the glasshouses, under a general foreman who was in charge of all departments, so acted as a deputy Head. I was told that our "duty" week would be one in three, and when on "duty" we were only allowed to leave the garden with permission from the Head. My wages would be twenty-eight shillings (£1.40) a week, plus four shillings when on "duty", and we were paid fortnightly.

Mr. Denning told me that Sir Felix's daughter spent a great deal of her time working in the garden, and she did her own floral work. I would, he said, certainly see a lot of her, so I must always be dressed neatly, wear a collar and tie, and never be seen in need of a shave. I could only remove my jacket if the weather was hot, and always be ready to put it back on if the lady came my way, and as a member of Sir Felix's staff I must wear an apron at all times.

I was in no position to object to these orders. I had only just arrived, and was only too pleased to have found a job so quickly. I had little chance of seeing much of the garden that day, but from what I did see I judged it to be very much smaller than were my last two situations. Even so, I felt I could usefully spend one or two years with Mr. Denning.

It was late afternoon when I returned to the bothy, and as my new mates came in for a meal I introduced myself to them. Fred Phelps was general foreman; he must have been about forty, and was by far the oldest man I had met in bothy. I was to share the second bedroom with him, while a young lad called Dennis, who was in the pleasure gardens, shared the first room with Terry from the kitchen garden. Fred was in charge of the bothy and did the food orders, which he told me usually came to around twelve shillings a week. The bothy lady would do my personal washing, which could cost me anything from one and six (7½p) to four shillings (20p).

No one went out that evening; it seemed there was nowhere much to go. There was a village some two miles away that could boast a public house, but little else, so we considered ourselves fortunate to have a wireless set which could be used either with earphones or a loudspeaker. True, we had to have one of our two low-tension wet batteries charged up every week, but this was done for us in the car garage by Sir Felix's chauffeur. A new high-tension dry battery had to be bought every few months; they cost about ten shillings (50p), so this was paid for by a heavy charge on the grub score.

This, my first evening, was almost entirely devoted to conversation and the wireless set did not come into use. As usual we each wanted to know about the gardens in which the others had worked. Fred gave a detailed account of the glories of Wollaton Hall in Nottinghamshire, where he had worked for some years. He had also been at Stourhead in Wiltshire, where it seems he spent most of his time working near, or even on, the large lake in that delightful garden, and at Leeds Castle in Kent, where there is also a great deal of water, so he was able to tell us of the wide range of aquatic plants he was familiar with. One expected a man of his age to have a wide experience of bothy life, and so he had; he told me this was the seventh bothy he had lived in, two of them being in Scotland and one in Ireland.

Hearing of Fred's wide range of experience made me feel that I was still very much a new boy, as this was only my third engagement away from home. Even so, my new friends seemed very interested in the gardens where I had been employed and I was able to add something to the evening's conversation.

All this was new to Dennis, as this was his first bothy, and he listened with interest to our descriptions of the different gardens we had worked in. Terry had worked at Blaize Castle, near Bristol, so he could join in to some extent.

We were up soon after six o'clock in the morning to get our breakfast and to start work at seven. When I asked how important time was in this garden Fred told me it was his job to see that no one was late in the mornings, as Mr. Perry seldom put in an appearance before the nine o'clock teabreak. This again was something new to me, as I had never before had a chance to stop work for a while between meals.

Fred then showed me the glass that was to be in my charge. First we went into the one vinery, then on into a peach and nectarine house where seven trees were growing. Next came a house of about one hundred carnations, and this led into three plant houses and a fernery. There were just over thirty heated frames, some of them set aside for the growing of melons and cucumbers. All this glass was heated from one boilerhouse, in which there were two Junior Robin Hood boilers, linked together so that we could have both on during a cold spell or only one if that should be sufficient. I saw no sign of any greenhouse temperature charts in any of the houses, which was rather pleasing.

Fred told me I would have to do all this on my own, but I could have the garden boy, Oliver, one or two days a week if he thought it necessary for me, or good for Oliver. I could see now that I was going to spend all my time propagating growing plants and fruit, so perhaps it was just as well that Sir Felix's daughter did her own flowers.

I was not unduly worried, because the amount of glass here was somewhat less than I had grown used to. It was not the number of plants I had to deal with that caused me any concern, but I could see that the quality did leave some scope for improvement.

After that I was taken around the pleasure grounds. A drive led up to the house, and to the right of the front door was an archway through a yew hedge forming the entrance to the rose garden. There were twelve beds of various shapes set in a lawn, each bed having one variety of rose, the whole being surrounded by a well-kept yew hedge.

From there we went into a heather garden around which was planted beech to form another hedge. This led on to an iris and herbaceous garden, surrounded by a hedge of cupressus, from which we came back to the large lawn that ran the length of the front of the "Big House". Crossing the lawn, we came to the shrub plantation, where each kind of shrub was planted en masse, to give a bold effect.

From there we went through a small wild garden to reach the kitchen garden. As usual there was a high wall around this garden, with my six lean-to glasshouses on the wall that faced south and east. The other walls supported trained fruit trees which were in the care of the kitchen garden staff.

Fred and I spent most of the morning looking around, so it was near dinner time when we got back to the bothy. There I met our bothy lady for the first time. She was a young person whose husband worked in the garden, so she was addressed as Mrs. Rogers; being around twenty-six she was hardly old enough to be called "Mum".

I had noticed that the bothy was spotlessly clean, so I was not surprised when she said she hoped I would be tidy, and would I please take off my dirty boots before I went into the bothy. She had a charming way of making her requests, so I could hardly take offence. Then she asked if she could call me by my first name, and this too I could hardly refuse.

I found our Mrs. Rogers to be very friendly. Later on she seemed a little too much so, and it gradually became obvious I would need to be very careful in my dealings with her, particularly as her husband and I became friends, working together as we did in the garden.

Fred, too, had warned me to watch my step with our Mrs. Rogers, as she seemed to be easily fascinated by any man, and we in the bothy were of necessity a bit too near to her for comfort at times. This was a great pity, as she was for the most part a very pleasant person, but it was realised that if any malicious gossip did arise in the bothy our employer would almost certainly be quite ruthless in dismissing the offending parties.

Sir Felix's daughter had been away when I started work at Verdley Place, so it was over three weeks before I met her. She came into the carnation house one morning, and for a time stood watching me disbud the flower stems. Then she introduced herself. She was a tall, somewhat buxom person, and obviously an outdoor type, with a tanned, almost red, face.

Wearing an old raincoat, and with a pair of rubber boots on her feet, she looked ready to do any kind of garden work. Indeed, that was what she proposed to do forthwith, and what was more, I was to help her for the rest of the morning. I was to leave what I was doing and go with her into one of the plant houses to restake some chrysanthemums she wanted to use up at the mansion, then I was to take them to the front door in a garden truck.

I was not allowed to go inside, but had to wait on the doorstep until she was ready. When one of the housemaids had put down a number of dust sheets it was my job to take these plants to make a bank of colour under the main stairway, covering the large pots with ferns.

Later that afternoon she and I were in the potting shed, potting geraniums and schizanthus, which I had started the day before. I was somewhat surprised to have to work alongside my employer, but she was well able to do any job that needed doing. I got a feeling she was taking note of the way I was doing my work, and I was not very happy at first with the idea of being watched, but as the day passed it gradually dawned on me that she was more concerned with my methods, and was perhaps even trying to get new ideas from me, so the day passed off quite well, as did many others later.

It soon became apparent to me that our Head was very subservient to Miss Schuster, as he was never far away when she was in the garden and would come running whenever she called. It was rather pathetic to see a Head Gardener so cowed down, and our employer took full advantage of the situation and made life very difficult for him at times.

Fred Phelps, too, was ever in awe of our Lady; this was one of the reasons he seldom left the bothy in the evenings, just in case he was needed. On a few occasions he asked me to stand by for him if he went out after working hours. When I pointed out that the "duty" man was always at hand he seemed to think that this was not good enough for Madam. I could see that I would have to stand on my own feet, as I would not be able to rely on either the Head or the general foreman for any support should I ever need it. I also felt quite certain that anything I said or did would come to the notice of Miss Schuster.

I have always given my employers due respect, but I had no intention of becoming subservient to anyone, and it was not too long before I found it necessary to assert some dignity. I was working in the vinery when I heard Miss Schuster calling me. I came down off some steps, walked to the door and out to where she was standing. "When I call you," she said, "you will not keep me waiting, you will run to me as quickly as possible." I stood quite still a little way from her.

I think I did this because I was to some extent taken aback. Then I said, "Madam, nature doesn't run, and we who work with nature must keep in step with our natural master." I had surprised myself by saying what I had, and I stood ready to receive a severe reprimand.

She looked at me for what seemed like minutes, and I began to wonder if she was waiting for an apology, but I said nothing. The waiting seemed endless, then she said I had better study nature in the carnation house and cut her some flowers. She was still waiting when I brought the blooms to her. She took them without a word, and I was left wondering if I had taken my dignity a little too far.

Talking about this incident over tea in the bothy, Fred was quite sure I would be dismissed at the end of the week, and I had a strong feeling he might be right. The following day Mr. Denning asked me what sort of a fool did I think I was, speaking as I did to our Lady. I tried to assure him that I had not been disrespectful in any way, but he said the matter would need careful consideration.

The following Friday was pay day, and I and everyone else was surprised and relieved to realise I had not been sacked. I felt more at ease after this episode, and even when working alongside Miss Schuster I felt I had nothing to worry about. I thought perhaps I might even have gained a little respect from her, as she never again suggested I might hurry.

I knew, though, that I could not stay long at Verdley Place. I was not learning very much, as there was not enough scope on this rather small estate. There was very little social life, and having no bus service we were rather cut off from meeting other people in the gardening fraternity, so once more I was getting an urge to move on, even though I had only been there a short while.

This desire to move received a real boost when Miss Schuster decided that we in the bothy were living too well and decreed that we were to be rationed for garden produce. Fred and I protested to Mr. Denning, but he would on no account go contrary to the orders given by our employer. Later he gave us a list of the vegetables we could have in any one week, and no fruit was to be supplied at all.

We pointed out that it would be very difficult for him to apply such a rule as we were living and working so close to the kitchen garden, but he made it plain to us that he would dismiss anyone who dared to break our employer's orders. Therefore we had our rations, and supplemented them in devious ways, but it did make some difference to our grub score, which moved over the thirteen shillings mark most weeks, and the fact that little was coming our way from the kitchen didn't help matters.

Then came an order that our coal was to be reduced to two tons a year. This did not create any great hardship as we could get plenty of wood, but we could see that there was an economy drive taking place and we wondered what would be reduced next. We did not have long to wait.

The following payday everyone's money was cut by two shillings and sixpence (12½p) a week, without any warning. We protested to the Head, only to be told that Sir Felix considered our living standards were too high as compared with industry. I suppose in some respects this might have been true, we did live very well, and no one was suffering any hardships in private service. We all had our difficulties and there was no way in which any of us could assert ourselves and at the same time keep our jobs, but to have had two pay cuts in less than a year was, I felt, just too much. There was nothing we could do about it, we had to accept things as they were, but in the bothy everyone decided to find another situation as soon as an opportunity arose.

We all did the usual things of writing to our past Head Gardeners and registering ourselves with the seed firms, but this time both Fred and I advertised in *The Gardener's Chronicle* under box numbers. It all seemed rather hopeless at the time, but my hopes rose some weeks later when Fred found his first Head's position on an estate near Cheltenham through the register of one of the seed firms. He considered himself rather fortunate to have found a situation where an unmarried Head was needed, and he got the job without an interview, which was most unusual. We wished him well, of course, but we never heard of him again after he left us.

I was tempted to apply for the now-vacant post, but I decided to do nothing as I felt I would gain very little by staying at Verdley Place for any length of time. On the Monday morning, however, I was summoned to see Miss Schuster in the morning room and was told I was promoted to the position of general and bothy foreman, with a rise of four shillings a week. I was not asked if I wanted the job, or even if I could do it; it appeared my promotion was an accomplished fact.

I said I would of course do my best to justify the trust put in me, but asked if Mr. Denning approved of this appointment. I was told he would have no objections.

Later on in the day I found Mr. Denning and told him of the substance of my interview with our employer. He seemed quite happy with the arrangement, but I still felt it was not right that a Head Gardener should have no say as to the appointment of his foreman.

Three weeks later a new man, Tom West, came to us from Hever Castle, one of the most important gardens in Kent. Tom came as inside journeyman in my old position, and soon proved himself to be a very useful young gardener, able to do the glasshouse work without much supervision. For a while things settled down again.

It was about that time that Mr. Denning bought himself a second-hand car. We were all very interested, and had some hopes we might even have a ride in it. This was not to be, however, as our employer was most displeased to think that any of his staff should have a motor-car, and his displeasure was made very clear to our Head.

He was not to be allowed to drive it on any of the roads on the estate, nor could he park it on the estate. This made things impossible for him, so as usual he bowed to his employer's wishes and sold the car, without ever having driven it.

I had been in my foreman's job for only three months when I had a letter from my old Head Gardener at Fonthill House, telling me there was a good job going at Gatton Park, at Reigate in Surrey, and he had recommended me to the Head Gardener, Mr. Richards. I was to go for an interview the following Monday without fail, as Mr. Mills had promised I would be there.

I was delighted at the thought of going to Gatton Park, as I knew it was one of the better gardens in the South, owned by Sir Jeremiah Colman, of mustard fame, and Lady Colman. That morning I went to Mr. Denning and told him I intended to go on this interview. He knew Gatton Park very well indeed, as he had at one time worked there as a journeyman, and he told me a great deal about the gardens there. He assured me it was a first-class establishment, but he was very concerned as to what Sir Felix would say when he knew I was looking for another post. He told me he could not guarantee that I could keep my job if I failed my interview, but he did say I could have the day off, provided I went without pay for that day.

I left the bothy early on the Monday morning to cycle to the station, where I took a train to Reigate. There I found I could get a bus to a point near Gatton Park; I then had to walk about half a mile to the lodge gates, and from there it was another mile up the drive to the garden gates. A man told me where the garden office was, and there I found four other men waiting to be interviewed. Mr. Richards was in his office with yet another man who, I assumed, had also applied for the situation.

I was by then more than a little worried about my chances of getting the job. The other men who were waiting were equally worried. We talked among ourselves, but each one of us knew that his chances were that much less because of the others. After about half an hour Mr. Richards came out, and seeing me he asked me my name. He told me to wait, then called one of the other men into the office. Twice more he came out and called a man into the office, then it was my turn.

First of all he read my references with considerable care. He knew from them where I had worked and what positions I had held, but he wanted to know what I knew about gardening. Looking up from the papers he started to ask me questions. I had to give a detailed account of my background and my family. That seemed to satisfy him.

The job he was offering, he said, was first journeyman of five in the plant and fruit houses; having been a foreman for three months, did I now wish to return to a journeyman's position? I assured him that, in a garden of the standard I could see around, I would be most happy to take the situation offered.

I was with him for almost half an hour. I think he was about to dismiss me, when he asked, "Can you play cricket?" That, I told him, was the one game I really did enjoy playing.

He then told me to go outside and wait, as he would want to see me again later. During the next hour he interviewed two other men, then I was called into the office once more. He just sat looking at me for a while, then said simply "You will start work here next Monday, and you will be in the bothy on Saturday afternoon."

Mr. Richards then gave me eight shillings interview expenses, but told me I would have to move at my own expense, and I could not expect to be met at the station on a Saturday. I felt that was the least of my worries.

I was walking on air as I left him and made my way back down the drive. How lucky I was to get the job in preference to all the other men who were there that day.

It was late in the evening when I called on Mr. Denning and gave him my written notice to terminate my employment with him. He accepted the fact that I was leaving, but wanted two weeks' notice, as we were paid fortnightly. I told him I could not stay after the coming Saturday, so he said he would see Miss Schuster, and she would have the last word.

The following day I had to report to the mansion, where I was shown into the morning room by the Butler, who told me I was to wait for Madam. Miss Schuster was very angry when she came into the room and gave me a lecture on my duties and loyalties to my superiors; I should be ashamed of myself for running away from a good employer and leaving her with the problem of finding another man.

I thought it wise to say very little, and I merely said that I had to look after my own future. She asked when I thought of leaving. When I told her I was due to move the following Saturday she said that was impossible, I must work out a full fortnight. When I told her that I was going as arranged with my new Head, and apologised for my early departure, she said that if I left on the Saturday there would be no wages paid that week; if I wanted my money I would have to stay for a second week. I was then curtly dismissed.

For the rest of that week I kept out of her way as much as possible. So it was that I lost a week's wages that I had already earned. Mr. Denning said there was nothing he could do about it, but he did wish me the very best of good fortune, and he did give me a very good reference and say that I could rely on him for help if ever I should need it.

# Heavy duty and cricket 13

I WAS able to beg a lift to Woking with my luggage, there to take a train to Reigate. I had to afford a taxi to complete my journey.

It was soon after noon when I arrived at Gatton Park on that Saturday in May. The bothy was above what I later discovered to be a laundry; again there was an outside stairway leading up to the entrance doors.

I went in to introduce myself to my new bothy mates, and received a welcome from Frank Bell, the foreman, who introduced me first to Clive Cooper, who was foreman in the pleasure gardens, then to his brother Jim, first journeyman in the kitchen garden. I also met Ken Barrett from the orchid houses and young Sam Frost, who would be my junior in the plant and fruit houses.

We sat down to dinner, with Frank at the head of the table and Clive at the far end, Jim and I on one side with Ken and Sam facing us. Here again the order of seating at the meal table reflected the position one held in the garden staff.

It was as well I left my unpacking until after the meal, as all the lads were in a hurry. Frank was obviously the "duty" man, as he sat with me at the table while the rest left to go into their bedrooms, soon to reappear one by one wearing cricket flannels. Now I realised why Mr. Richards had asked me if I played cricket; it seemed that everyone here did.

The lads were quickly away, so Frank and I had a chance to get to know each other, which was very important as, he being my foreman, we would be working together most of the time. He told me that everyone in the bothy was expected to play cricket; I probably realised then that Mr. Richards only engaged staff in the bothy who were good at their job and could also play his favourite game.

Our employer, Sir Jeremiah Colman, had his own cricket team, of which Mr. Richards was captain when Sir Jeremiah was not playing, so we were all expected to be quite useful on the field. As workers, we had to attend to all the ground work and to prepare the wickets in our own time. Sir Jeremiah supplied all the gear. This kind of arrangement suited us very well, though there was one small disadvantage—we could not offer our services to any other club and expect to remain on the staff.

After clearing away, Frank showed me around the bothy. The room in which we had been sitting was quite large: it had the usual table and chairs for six people, the inevitable dresser on one wall, and a sink and draining board. At one end of the room there was a door to a walk-in larder, and a second door into Frank's bedroom. Down the long wall across from the dresser were three more doors, each leading into a bedroom, while at the other end was the entrance into which I had come earlier, and the black cooking range. There was an annexe at the bottom of the stairs for bicycles, and this also served as a woodshed. Beyond that was the water toilet.

Two hanging oil lamps supplied the lighting in the main room. These were very important, since there was only one window, which was over the sink, so the greater part of this room had very little daylight. Frank showed me into the four bedrooms, two of them with only a single bed each set aside for the foremen. In each of the other rooms there were two beds, with a chest of drawers for each person; by the side of each bed was a cane chair and a little bedside chest, provided because there was no sitting room where one could read or write. All of the floors were covered with lino, but there were mats at the side of each of the old iron beds. This bothy compared favourably with the others I had lived in, and I was quite happy with what I had seen.

Frank and I talked for a while about our hours of work and our pay and similar matters of great interest to a newcomer to the bothy. He told me our hours were from seven in the morning until half past five for most of the year, but for six weeks either side of Christmas we left off an hour earlier. We came into the bothy for half an hour at nine o'clock each morning for our breakfast, and again at half past noon for the half-hour dinner break.

On Saturdays everyone stopped at midday, a concession that was to some extent because of the cricket, but from September to May we worked on until half past one. He knew my wages were thirty-one shillings a week, but he was able to tell me that we received an extra six shillings when on "duty".

I was to do what was called "heavy duty": this meant attending to the five boilers, doing most of the weekend and all of the evening watering that might need doing, opening and closing the many greenhouses as necessary, and raising or lowering the many

**The bedrooms at Gatton Court, drawn here by Toni Goffe, compared favourably with the others I had lived in.**

woodlath blinds used for shading the glasshouses in summer and helping to conserve heat in the winter.

There were four of us doing "heavy duty" in turn, and we each had a "light duty" man to help us at weekends. These men were paid four shillings for their part in the "duty". Bothy "charges", as they were called there, came one week in six, which ensured we all did our share of the work. The lads at Gatton Park were very helpful to the "charge" man, and the work in the bothy was shared to a considerable extent.

After we had had a long talk Frank proceeded to wash up the dinner tableware. I offered to help, and this was accepted. When we had done that he suggested I went over to the cricket field, as he had work to do in the garden, but he promised to show me around the next day.

I found my way to the ground quite easily. It was a lovely setting for cricket, the playing area was open on three sides which meant the light was good for play, but a row of oak trees along the top side of the ground gave all the shade that was needed, and the thatched pavilion tucked under the trees was quite charming. I settled down to watch what turned out to be a very good game; I could see that I would need to play very well to hold a place in this team.

After tea the home side were to bat, and Mr. Richards seeing me there came over to where I was standing. I think he realised who I was, but he had forgotten my name, so in a way I had to reintroduce myself. He made a few comments about the bothy and the job I had come to do, but at that time he was more interested in the cricket. He questioned me once again about my ability on the field and asked what I knew about the rules of cricket. I suppose he was reasonably satisfied with my answers, since a little later he told me to go out and stand as umpire for the rest of the game. Fortunately I had very little to do and no real decisions to make, but standing there on this, my first day with total strangers, and knowing I was being watched by my new Head, I was more than a little nervous. It was the first time I had been called upon to umpire in a match, and I was very thankful when the time came to leave the field.

Clive, Jim and Ken had been playing that day, so after the match we got to know each other better over a glass of beer in what was supposed to be our local, though it was over a mile away. The pub, which was quite modern, had two bars, private and public, with a taproom for off sales. Fred and Freda, known to everyone as the Two Fs, made everyone welcome, including ladies in the private bar, which boasted a cushion on every seat, so it was almost a pleasure to pay the extra ha'penny on each drink.

We got back to the bothy well after ten o'clock, so I went into my bedroom to unpack most of my things and prepare for bed. When I went back into the living room, however, I was surprised to see all the lads having supper, so I joined them in my first-ever late night meal in a bothy.

Most of the next day was taken up by a tour of the glasshouses and garden. First of all I had to see the glass that I was to have in my care. There were four peach houses containing twenty-one peach and nectarine trees, two eighty-foot vineries with five vines in one and four in the other, two houses for the growing of pot plants, one fernery and the very large flowering house. To this house most of the plants were brought as they came into flower, and they were staged for effect as this was one of the focal points that Sir Jeremiah liked to show his guests.

Of course, many of the plants from here were taken up to the house, only to be replaced by others, so everything in there had to be spotless at all times. The red-tiled floor was washed down twice every day after the watering had been done, and then mopped dry. The brass door handles were polished every day, and the hot water pipes were blacked over every month to contrast with the low white walls; I was even told I would have to wash the shingle that the plants stood on at least once a month. That was the one house we could not fumigate without Sir Jeremiah's permission, in case he had any of his guests walking in the garden.

Frank had only three houses in his care. In his orchard house were growing pears, plums, cherries, figs and oranges, all in pots or tubs, and apricots trained on a back wall. A door through that wall led into the hot pineapple annexe. In his two carnation houses were some five hundred carnation plants and a long row of propagating frames for the many cuttings that were taken each year. We also went through the seven houses which were in Sam's charge. He had melon and cucumber houses, a large tomato and chrysanthemum house, and three more where he had pot plants and alpines. The three of us were to work together as a team, with the help of an old man called Josh and Keith Vexley, the inside garden boy.

I was taken through twelve orchid houses, some of them quite small where the orchids were propagated and grown when very young. Most of the young orchids were grown from seed, sown in small air-tight growing bottles. The hybridising was done by an orchid grower, but Sir Jeremiah had a considerable say in what crosses were made. As these seedlings grew they were moved into the larger growing houses, and when these came into flower, sometimes years later, they were displayed in a large orchid flower house together with many picture plants and other unusual, mostly tropical, plants. This was another focal point in this superb garden, a feature everyone had to see.

Six people were employed to grow these orchids. The orchid grower had a foreman, three journeymen and a boy, and I was surprised to learn that one of the journeymen was in fact a woman called Jenny. It was strange to find myself in a garden geared to employ women.

The kitchen garden was quite extensive. The six men employed there were obviously kept busy, as they had not only outdoor vegetables to provide but were growing many tender or early plants in their two vegetable houses. I saw potatoes, dwarf beans, peppers and gherkins growing in pots, and the borders planted with runner beans, peas, lettuce and other salad plants. Nearby and underground were the mushrooms and forcing cellars.

The whole of the glasshouses and kitchen garden area was again surrounded by the usual high wall. Some of the glasshouses were built on to the wall as lean-to structures, but the greater part of the walls was given over to the growing of trained fruit trees. Two men spent most of their time tending to these trees and to the two

**Toni Goffe's drawing of the Gatton Park bothy, which was above a laundry and was reached by a set of steps.**

orchards, which were almost a mile from the glass but close to a wild garden, where these men filled in their time.

After seeing all that we went back to the bothy, where Clive was doing the "charge" work. With a little help from the lads he had cooked a very good midday meal.

After lunch Frank had obtained permission to show me the gardens around the mansion, which was a large, almost square building with an interior courtyard. In the centre of the enclosure a fountain was playing, and around and about were some two dozen large tubs filled with shrubs and small trees.

We left the house by way of a formal rose garden big enough to accommodate over two thousand bush, shrub and climbing roses. From there we went across an expanse of lawn with some lovely cedar trees, most of which were Lebanon cedars, though there were two perfect specimens of blue Atlantica.

After walking the length of this huge mansion we came to an area of informal garden, with herbaceous plants in beds and shrubs set in grass, and then to the Japanese garden with fascinating little bridges over a winding stream fed from a natural spring. Acers, small conifers, irises, primulas and many other small plants were muddled together, making a really delightful picture.

From the Japanese garden we moved on into the shrub and bulb garden, where lilies would be a feature later in the year, past some topiary work in clipped yew, box and holly along both sides of a grass walk. Of all the shapes into which the bushes had been trimmed the most original were the two box bushes clipped and shaped to make a full-sized man. Or was it perhaps the yew settee?

Then I was able to enjoy a large rock garden, carefully placed to fall away and merge into the water garden, which was on three sides of a small lake. A short walk through what was known as the berberis beds and we arrived at the wild garden, where plants grew quite naturally, though even so there was nothing untidy or unkempt about it.

During my tour around this large and fascinating garden I had been making mental notes of all kinds of things. I gathered that I was now one of thirty-five gardeners employed there, though Frank told me that the number varied a bit from time to time. When we got back to the glasshouses it was time for Frank to attend to the boilers. Here, too, cleanliness was of great importance, and having cleaned and refuelled the fires Frank carted away the ashes and brushed the boilers and floor clean. When we left the whole place was spotless, just in case Sir Jeremiah wished to show any of his many friends around the working parts of the garden such as the boiler houses, the potting sheds and the tool houses. He often did.

I had spent a valuable day with Frank, and I thought I might spend the evening looking around part of the estate, but this was not to be. I was informed by my room-mate Ken that we were expected to go to church on Sunday evenings, so I considered it prudent to do so. The church was really part of the mansion, built into the south-west corner of the house. It was very beautiful inside, and the evening sunlight shining through a lovely stained glass window at the west end cast a multitude of colours on the fifty or so pews. There was a balcony along the length of one side containing private pews for the use of the Colman family and their guests.

The priest was a young man retained by Sir Jeremiah to take services on Sundays and Holy days. Communion was taken on Monday mornings for the start of a new week, and everyone who worked on the estate and wished to take Communion was given time on Mondays from seven until half past to attend church. On my first working day I never gave the church a thought, being keen to make a start in my new charge.

We left the bothy a little before seven. My first job after unlocking and opening some ventilators in my glasshouses was to go with Frank up to the house. We loaded several flowering plants, ferns and cut flowers to carry them up to the mansion, where we went into the large flower room, which contained everything one could need to do floral work. Changing into house slippers, Frank got permission from the Butler, Mr. Leader, for us to go through the green baize door into the main rooms to attend to any watering or rearranging of flowers that was necessary.

I would have liked to have stopped to look at the stupendous decor of these beautiful rooms, but that would have to wait until we had more time since we were supposed to be finished by eight o'clock, when members of the family would probably be around. We learnt from Mr. Leader that the dining table that evening would be without a cloth, so we could use white or pastel shade flowers for our table centre; they would reflect well in the highly polished table.

It was not until after our midday meal that one of us would go back to the house to put on the new table centre. We would have to satisfy Mr. Leader that our flowers were suitable for his table, and only when we had done so were we permitted to go into the dining room to set our display. This was always a job that needed great care, for to spill a drop of water on to a newly laid table was a cardinal sin.

We were perhaps looking for a spread of something over four feet, and at times this did cause us problems in getting these plants through the greenhouse door and up to the mansion. There were several large bronze tubs and big porcelain bowls which needed special plants to fill them. The back of an upright piano in Lady Colman's boudoir would have been very obvious on entering the room but for a flower basket, four feet long and only nine inches wide, with an arched handle from end to end. For this, too, we needed specially produced plants that would fit into the container, fill the whole basket and cover the back of the piano.

This was a growing art I had not encountered before, and a lot of thought had to be given to keeping up a continuity of these special plants throughout the year. A great deal of preparation was done by careful staking as the plants were growing, then getting them into their proper place in the rooms needed considerable thought as well as some assistance from the inside staff.

Mr. Leader was in charge of everyone employed in the house, and we came under his control the moment we entered the mansion. He was, perhaps, the most important person on the whole estate, being in very close contact with Sir Jeremiah and Lady Colman. He had three footmen directly under him as well as a house boy and an elderly man everyone knew as Boots. Mrs. Simpson, the Housekeeper, had six housemaids and two girls in the laundry to supervise, and Mrs. Ploit, the Cook, employed two kitchen maids, two more maids in the scullery and two girls in the still room. The head chauffeur was a Mr. Bakewell, and as he had four cars and a van in the garage his second man, Tom, and his understudy Philip must have had a lot of driving and maintenance work to do.

It was at breakfast on my first working day that I met Mrs. Smart, our bothy "Mum", a person of middle age and, I was not surprised to learn, a widow. She lived in one of the estate houses with her two daughters, Nelly, one of the housemaids working under Mrs. Simpson, and Molly, the younger, who was employed in the laundry. From the first I got the feeling that Mrs. Smart was a real "Mum" to us in the bothy, and this proved to be correct in many different ways. She had decided that as Molly worked in the laundry there was no reason why she should not do our personal washing, which I thought was a bit hard on the girl until I realised that we gave her a present from time to time, usually in the form of chocolates.

Most mornings "Mum" came in to light the fire just before seven to make sure "her boys" had a good breakfast when we returned later; if Frank or I were delayed up at the house doing our floral work the meal would be waiting for us when we got back. She took it upon herself to see that our cricket gear was clean and pressed ready for the Saturday matches. She really took a pride in keeping "her boys" smart, and when we went out at weekends or in the evenings we just could not let "our Mum" down. She liked a glass of Guinness, which was why there were always six bottles of Guinness on the grub score; and of course she was kept well supplied with garden produce.

Wednesday was cricket practice night, so with the rest of the lads I had two hours in the nets. Mr. Richards joined us, and I could tell he was watching me rather carefully. He was quite a useful bowler and set me a few problems until I got used to his spin. Once I did get the measure of that spin I knew that if I had some patience

I could hit some of his deliveries. I also had a bowl at him, and managed to keep him quiet. At the end of the evening's workout I was told I would be considered for the next Saturday's game.

Our Head was team manager, and it was he that chose the men who played. This was something very unusual. I suppose I had done well enough, as my name was on the team sheet for the next match. We were beaten that day, but I had quite a successful debut, making twenty-seven runs and managing to hold two catches that came my way.

After each game we had to have the usual drink with our opponents, together with the inquest, which would continue when we were back in the bothy. Of course I was happy to join in, but I found even greater pleasure when the conversation at the meal table turned to gardening and gardens.

Each of us would tell the others about the estates on which we had worked, and for the most part everyone was keen to listen. Frank was ever willing to talk about Knowsley Hall in Lancashire, where he had started his training. This was apparently a large estate and a leading garden in the North, a fine place to have done one's training, but when he got around to telling us about his two years at Blenheim Palace we really became fascinated. He had also had two years at Berkeley Castle, down in Gloucestershire, so he was able to tell us a great deal of the history of that old fortress and of the quite tender plants growing there between the buttresses of the round shell keep built by Robert Fitzharding in the 1150s.

Jim Cooper had come to Gatton Park from Chatsworth in Derbyshire, the home of the Duke of Devonshire, whose superb gardens are legendary. He told us that the feature of those gardens was the fountains working from the natural pressure of the water brought down from the hill above the mansion. He could also tell us of the many happenings at Clivedon, beside the Thames, and of the many famous people who were guests at that fashionable mansion.

I suppose it was to be expected that Ken Barrett's main interest was orchids, since he had specialised in orchids and was very good at his job. He was not greatly interested in what the rest of us were doing, but he did sometimes talk about his year in Spain.

Clive was very different, he was always keen to know what everyone was doing and what they had done; he often said he would be a Head Gardener before any of us. He had started his gardening at Townhill Park in Hampshire, as did his brother later, before moving down to Exbury, on the Beaulieu River just about opposite the famous old shipbuilding centre of Bucklers Hard. There he worked in the vast collection of flowering shrubs and rhododendrons for which Exbury is famous, but before coming to us he had been working at Wilton House, not far from Salisbury, mainly under glass.

During these conversations I learnt a great deal about the many bothies my compatriots had lived in. Some of them were obviously quite good, and it was well worth remembering those estates where the bothy was good and the garden was interesting, with a good Head. On the other hand there were still some rather poor bothies around. I suppose that most, like the one we were living in, were adequate, if not exactly comfortable.

For the most part we all enjoyed our life in the bothy. To a considerable extent it was a life that had its freedom, except perhaps during "duty" weeks, so we didn't really mind being kept on our toes most of the time, and the companionship was something to cherish. Of course we did not always see eye to eye with each other, but I never encountered any bad feeling between any of us in the bothy. We were a unit, and we were always prepared to help each other, which made it all the more painful when we learned from outside the bothy that Ken Barrett was in fact a married man.

At first none of us would entertain such an idea, but the rumour persisted and sooner or later the matter would have to be cleared up. We all knew Ken was courting a local girl; this was quite usual, so nobody gave it any thought. Ken and I shared our bedroom and we had much in common, often talking late into the night, so when one night he asked me if I would like to buy his portable gramophone we made a deal; for two pounds I acquired the gramophone and his small collection of records.

There were several other items he wanted to sell, among them his cricket sweater and white flannels. He said he intended leaving Gatton Park shortly and would no longer need them, so again we paid little heed to this sudden need for money. I also knew that at weekends when not on "duty" he did not return to the bothy on Saturday evenings, but I paid no attention to that either, as he quite freely told us he was staying with his girl friend, and that was none of our business.

The matter came to a head when Frank, as foreman in the bothy, called Clive and me into his bedroom one evening and asked us what we knew about these rumours. Was Ken married? We could not be certain, but we had to admit that, thinking about the things he was selling and his sudden need for money, the rumour could well be true. Frank decided that he would have to put the matter directly to Ken, which he did in the privacy of our bedroom. Ken admitted that he had had to get married, and had done so two months earlier.

Now this put us in a dilemma. If we told the Head Gardener we knew that my room-mate would almost certainly get the sack, but on the other hand if we did not report the matter we would be breaking one of the first rules of bothy life, which was that bothies were provided for unmarried men while training to be gardeners. There was the code of conduct subscribed to by all bothy men to support each other at all times, yet we would be stirring up trouble for ourselves if nothing was said.

After some discussion Frank decided that it was his duty to inform Mr. Richards. Ken agreed that there was nothing else Frank could do; he said that in any case he was tired of living a life of deception.

The matter was reported to the Head the following morning. To say that Mr. Richards was annoyed is to put it mildly. He wanted to know how long he had been kept in ignorance of this deceit; when he was told that we had found out only the previous evening he became a little more composed, but he was still very angry.

He immediately sent for Ken to attend him in the office. What passed in there we never knew, but Ken was given a week's wages and told to be out of the bothy before nightfall. To be fair to Mr.

Richards, he did give Ken a good reference regarding his work.

When we returned to the bothy for lunch that day our compatriot was already packed and ready to move out, and "Mum" was in tears. It was a sad occasion for all of us. We wished Ken well as he left, but it was rather a futile thing to do as none of us could help him in any way. He did say he would let us know how he got on, but this was a promise he probably felt he did not need to keep.

That evening Mr. Richards made one of his rare visits to the bothy. He gave us a lecture on what was expected from the men living in his bothy and made it very clear what would happen to any of us who dared to break the understood code of conduct expected to be observed in bothies everywhere.

Nearly two months passed before Bill Sanger came to join us from Longleat, the Marquess of Bath's estate in Wiltshire. He took Ken's position in the orchid houses and became my new room-mate. He was twenty, and had three years' experience of bothy life. Bill was a likeable fellow and we became firm friends, but it soon became clear that he found the going hard as he tried to keep up the standards of his predecessor.

# Exotic plants 14

AS THE weeks passed by I was able to see more of this large estate. There was a lodge at each of the four entrances, and all of them were at least a mile from the mansion.

The estate employees occupied the twenty-two houses in Gatton village and in the cottages on the three farms, forty-three dwellings in all. The five maintenance men had their own workshops and were mainly employed on estate work, but at times they were hired out to neighbouring farms to do repairs. One of these men was a blacksmith, and he was in great demand in the area for repairing the now-popular farm tractors and other machinery and for making new parts for them.

It was he who made and fitted a new cooking range in the bothy, the open firebox being big enough to burn quite large logs. "Mum" was very pleased with her new range, which had a large oven and two hotplates. We were promised all kinds of different dishes, but that did not last long as we were not too keen on increasing our grub score, which kept reasonably steady at around thirteen shillings. That included "Mum's" Guinness, plus a little which we put aside to buy "Mum" her Christmas present.

In September Mr. Richards paid another visit to the bothy, this time to tell us that he and other Head Gardeners in the district had formed a Gardeners' Mutual Improvement Society that was to meet in Reigate every other Monday evening during the winter months. He expected us all to join, and to attend regularly.

We could see this might well be a good thing for us to join, so we all agreed to do so. After all, it was perfectly clear that we really had no choice in the matter, but we were somewhat taken aback when he told us that we would be paying a subscription of one pound for the first year, just to get the society on its feet; after the first year it was hoped we would need to subscribe much less than that. There were quite a few comments about having to pay so much, but we were told we should be proud to be founder members of the new organisation.

As it turned out the society proved to be a great success. For one thing it enabled us to meet regularly with men from two other bothies, and we were also meeting other Head Gardeners from the district, and this was always a good thing to be able to do. There were thirteen of us who were living in bothies. The men from the other bothies were, like us, a little sore at having to pay a pound to join, but they too had been told rather than asked to join.

However expensive it was for us, we knew it was a splendid idea to get the society going. After a while a number of good amateur gardeners began to attend the meetings, and their views on gardening were usually well worth listening to and we gained a lot of useful information, which we knew must help us in our careers.

I think it is safe to say we enjoyed going to these meetings as there was not a great deal to do in the dark evenings. It was possible to cycle into Reigate and go to the pictures and to the occasional dance, but nobody seemed very keen to go far after a day's work, so we spent a lot of time reading or playing cards. Bill Sanger was very popular, as he taught us to play Bridge properly; playing for tuppence a hundred, the games were keen but nobody lost very much money.

"Mum" decided to do something for "her boys" during the dark evenings and organised an occasional party at her house. She would invite some of her daughters' girl friends and we would go along, taking something to drink, while "Mum" supplied some food. Those were good evenings, and everyone enjoyed dancing to records and playing party games, our hostess making sure that we and the girls were well mixed. She tried very hard, but poor "Mum" was a little bit disappointed that no romances started from her efforts.

The "duty" man could not leave the bothy for these evenings, he would have to be on hand to attend to the boilers and to keep a close check on the temperatures in the many glasshouses, so he would often be on his own in the evenings. As it so happened, quite a few mice frequented our bothy; we possessed an air pistol, and it became something of a competition to see who could shoot the most mice when "duty" man; the best I can remember was a bag of four, by Clive. We didn't want to thin the mice population too much, so we made a point of feeding our little victims so they would go on breeding, or at least encourage more mice to invade our home, for the dubious pleasure of the "duty" man.

Our Saturdays were for the most part taken up by Sir Jeremiah's shooting parties, since all who could be spared from the gardens and farms were required to go beating. As the shoots usually went on until around four o'clock we were paid three shillings to compensate us for the afternoon's overtime. Lunch was the usual meat sandwiches and beer, taken wherever we happened to be after the second or third drive. The beating parties varied between forty and sixty men, according to the number of guests invited to the shoot. The four gamekeepers bred hundreds of pheasants and partridges; on what was called a good day as many as four hundred birds would be killed, together with many hares, which were plentiful on the estate, as were rabbits.

With the training I had received at Fonthill House I became chief poacher. This is not entirely true, as we had permission from the Head Gamekeeper to catch rabbits for our table, but on occasion we did enjoy roast bird or jugged hare, which was "Mum's" speciality.

As Christmas drew near I could see that I would be "on the wheel" over the holiday. I was informed that the "light duty" man was excused Christmas "duty", one man being enough to do all that was necessary. I was also told that there would be no presents from Sir Jeremiah, so at least we would be spared the ritual of going up to the mansion to meet our employer and his family. Perhaps this was because the family went to Scotland each Christmas and stayed over the New Year; this I could well understand when I learnt that Lady Colman came from Arbroath.

Some of the indoor staff were taken to Scotland for the Christmas season. The Butler took one footman and three housemaids with him, and the Cook took two kitchen maids, leaving

Mrs. Simpson in charge of the mansion for the three weeks they were away.

As was usual in all bothies "Mum" had her present from us. From the saving we had done throughout the year we were able to give her nearly five pounds.

I was a little concerned for myself when I knew "Mum" and the girls were going away for the holiday. I also knew the lads would either be going home or to friends for the four days, as Christmas Eve was on the Sunday that year. There was no doubt about it, I was going to be on my own in the bothy, and I was not looking forward to Christmas at all. There were some books I had not read, but it seemed likely I was going to spend some time "mouse shooting".

Mr. Richards had come into the bothy on the Saturday to see who was taking the "duty" and to make sure everyone knew they must be back on Tuesday evening at the latest. There were plenty of trains running over the holiday, so no excuses would be entertained for lateness. I was kept busy on the Sunday, Christmas Eve, attending to the boilers and the glasshouses, but being on my own the time passed very slowly.

We had not bought any special fare on the grub score, and what we did have I thought I would have to prepare myself, but "Mum" had not forgotten. She had made two small puddings, iced a cake and prepared quite a few vegetables and some fruit, and I was given detailed instructions what to do with all the prepared food.

Christmas morning post brought me more good things from my mother, and with a present from Dorothy I felt reasonably happy to start the holiday period. The few minutes I had with the postman on Christmas morning was a pleasing interlude, and the day passed quickly enough doing my work and cooking "Mum's" dishes, but the evening dragged slowly away and "mice shooting" gave me no pleasure.

Boxing Day was, for me, much better. Frank and Sam returned in time to prepare a midday meal, and one by one they all arrived back by early evening. I was pleased to see them, but I don't suppose they were particularly happy to be back as we all knew we were about to start on our really busy season.

We were getting some of the plants and seeds from the Kingdon Ward expedition in Eastern Europe and Southern Asia, which was rather exciting as these were plants about which we knew little or nothing. There were notes with most of the plants and seeds telling us which order of plant life they were thought to come under, and some were already named. Others had just a number, and in those cases all we had to go on was information on the terrain, the soil and the temperature where these plants had been found growing.

We were delighted to be one of the gardens where these new plants were to be grown for the first time, and as the seeds germinated and the plants started into new growth they had every possible attention. Of course we made some mistakes, as was only to be expected, but we did manage to grow a wide range and everyone was keenly interested. Some of the plants turned out to be of little value, and others were nondescript. Those that were considered to be of some value or of interest to growers and botanists were sent to Kew Gardens for further trials before they could be recommended to go into general culture.

Besides dealing with these new species we were growing a wide range of plants, including orchids, to be ready for the big spring and summer shows. We had been allocated a thirty-foot frontage at the Chelsea Flower Show and everyone was determined to make a success of this, so there were no grumbles when we were called upon to do extra work in the evenings and at weekends. Although we received no extra money for the extra work, preparing for these shows must have cost a great deal of money, yet nobody seemed to consider the expense.

We knew that Mr. Richards had to keep some sort of budget, but we also knew that he made quite sure he overspent in order to ensure that his allowance would not be cut the following year. This was noticeable in the way we were encouraged to burn anthracite, even though at times it did not seem necessary to keep all the boilers going the way we did. Although we used most of the flowerpots twice or three times we did very little washing of pots; if they did get a bit dirty they were smashed and new ones were bought. As for bamboo canes, they were used only three or four times before being burned. This kind of expense seemed quite unnecessary, but then of course the tradesmen our Head dealt with could be generous to him if they were getting good orders.

As May got nearer more and more of our time was spent attending to the many plants we were going to exhibit at Chelsea. These were carefully staked and tied to present a front to each plant; some were potted on, to give the plant a slight check to get it to perfection on the day, and others were subjected to a higher temperature to bring them on or were perhaps kept cool to get the timing just right.

The week before the show the whole exhibit was put together on the staging in my flowering house, as Mr. Richards put it, to get the many plants to grow together as a unit for a few days. And this they did, of course, though I think the staging was really done to impress Sir Jeremiah and to get his comments.

Sunday was packing day, and everyone was on hand to pack our treasures with the utmost care into specially made cases. Each plant was packed individually, and in many cases each flower on a plant had its own support. The cases were loaded on to a large motor-van, which left the garden in the late afternoon with Mr. Richards, the orchid grower and the two foremen from the bothy, Frank and Clive. They knew they would have to work late into the night and all day on Monday with hardly a stop for meals, staging our exhibit ready for Tuesday, when members of the Royal Family were expected to tour the show. It was left to me to put the flowering house back into some semblance of order for the next few days, and Bill Sanger took charge of the orchid houses.

Two members of the garden staff were to be on duty at our stand throughout the show. My turn came on Thursday. We were each given a free pass into the Royal Hospital grounds, where the show is held, and we had an allowance of seven shillings and sixpence to cover our expenses for the day.

What a day to remember that was. The questions from the public never seemed to end; there were times when we had difficulty in understanding what the many foreign visitors were saying, but we did our best to reply to everyone's questions. It was fortunate for me that my companion for the day was Jenny from the orchid houses, as she was able to answer the many queries concerning the orchids; by this time I had become well acquainted with all the other plants we were showing.

We had the chance to speak to quite a few celebrities in the garden world, and I was particularly pleased to meet Mr. Mills again. Sir Jeremiah paid us a visit, making sure that all was well with his exhibit, and Mr. Richards came to see that Jenny and I were managing to cope.

All this was very exciting, and so very new to me. What pleased me most was that my father came to our stand; I had written to tell him which day I was to be at Chelsea, and as he always had one day at the show he decided to come on the day when I was detailed to attend. Jenny said she could manage the stand if I wanted to have an hour or so with my dad, so I was able for the first time ever to take my dad out to lunch. We spent well over my hour together looking at all the wonderful exhibits at this greatest of all shows, and the time soon came when I had to get back to relieve Jenny so that she too could enjoy this wonderland of colour and beauty. By the evening, when we made our way back by train to Reigate, we were very tired, but happy to have played our small part in such a great exhibition.

Our plants returned on Friday evening, and all of us from the bothy spent the weekend getting everything back into its right glasshouse where each plant was to be kept growing in readiness for the Royal Show in June. Quite a lot of the plants would be needed a second time; we would still have orchids, but in the main this was to be an exhibit of greenhouse plants and vegetables.

This time I was given a chance to help with the staging, as Frank was unwell. Now I realised just how clever Mr. Richards was at putting an exhibit together; somehow he seemed always to have the right plant in the right place, at the right time. I took careful note of the way he did things; I was learning fast, and my new knowledge was to serve me well later in the year as we were to stage two exhibits at the Royal Horticultural Hall in July and October.

Jenny and I were together again at the Royal Show in June, but somehow that didn't seem to have the same appeal that Chelsea had had, perhaps because it was in the main an agricultural show. Even so, the standard in the horticultural tents was very high, and Sir Jeremiah was particularly pleased with our exhibit as it won him a silver medal.

A week after the Royal Show we were all given something of a surprise. Sir Jeremiah decided that as it was becoming a custom in industry for men to have a week's paid holiday everyone on the estate should have a week off with full pay. We were all delighted at the news. Not one of us in the bothy had ever had a paid holiday before, so we had to think up plans for making use of this holiday week when it came.

It was left to heads of departments to decide when their staff could take this time off, and Mr. Richards came into the bothy to see the "duty" rota so that he could tell us the dates we could have. Frank, being bothy foreman, was the first to go; we were all rather pleased about that, as he was still far from well and we hoped the break might see him fit once more.

My turn came in late July, and like most of the lads I went home; I was able to get away on the Saturday and could return on the following Sunday, so I was going to be home for almost eight whole days. I was so pleased to see my parents once more; I had not seen my mother for a very long time, so I received quite a welcome from her. I also had quite a greeting from Dorothy when I met her again.

My father was keenly interested in the growing I had been doing and in how my methods had changed in the few years I had been away. I spent a great deal of that week with him in his garden, meeting Dorothy and many of my old school friends in the evenings. We had one lovely evening when I took my parents and Dorothy out for an evening meal; it made me very happy to know that she and my parents were pleased to be in each other's company. I felt that the one pound five shillings and threepence the meal cost was money well spent.

Sunday came all too soon. I was able to get an afternoon train back to Reigate so as to be in the bothy that evening. One by one we all took our holiday, until in the late summer it was Bill Sanger's turn to have his week, but he had nowhere to go. We now learnt that he had no parents, nor had he any relations, and that as far as he knew he had spent all his early life in an orphanage.

Had we thought about it we might have realised he was all on his own in the world, as he never received any letters or mail of any kind. Now we were left to wonder where he had spent the last Christmas, but Bill never enlightened us. Perhaps none of us thought it was any of our business, so we hadn't asked him, but now we decided it was time somebody did make it their business and with Bill's approval Frank, Jim and I wrote to our parents to ask if any of them would take Bill for his week's holiday. By return of post he had three invitations, and all of our parents were anxious to have him and to make him really welcome, so now his problem was which of the three invitations to accept. Bill just didn't know what to do, and for the first time in my life I saw a man cry just because someone wanted him.

He was quite unable to decide, so we solved his dilemma by the cut of a pack of cards. Having thus left the decision to chance, we were able to tell him that he was to spend his holiday with Jim's parents in Reading. I think the best thing that happened in the bothy that year was seeing a big grin on Bill's face when he returned.

Our cricket team had not done very well that summer, as the shows and then the holidays had taken up quite a lot of our Saturdays, and now we were to lose one of our best young players. Mr. Richards had decided the time had come for Sam Frost to move on, and he had found a place for him as first journeyman at Warwick Castle. A young man from there, Neil Samson, was coming to us as a replacement. Neil was only sixteen, and this was his first bothy. What did surprise us was the fact that he had never played cricket, and didn't think he would be interested in the game.

Neil was a good lad and worked well, but it took him a long time to settle down to his new life. He was homesick for weeks, and made himself quite ill; had it not been that his father was able to come to visit him on a couple of Saturdays he would almost certainly have gone back home. He did settle down in time, however, but he was hardly the type of person to take kindly to bothy life.

With the coming of autumn there were to be considerable changes in the garden. Sir Jeremiah had been in Scotland most of September as a guest with some shooting parties, and on his return he decided to enlarge the garden as he was not satisfied with things as they were, having visited some of the better estates in Scotland. He was not the sort of man to be satisfied with anything but the best. His garden had to be as good as, or better than, any of those he had visited, and what he wanted he would have; expense was no object.

This rivalry between the owners of large estates was much appreciated by the garden staff, as we in turn liked to boast about our gardens when with our contemporaries.

A contractor was engaged to remake and enlarge the rock garden under the supervision of Sir Jeremiah and Mr. Richards. Tons of large rocks, and many smaller ones, were used to make this a large and impressive rock garden that was planned to merge gradually into its surroundings. On one side it ran down towards a new lake and on the other the rocks would bit by bit be lost into a small wood, the rocks getting smaller and less closely spaced as one neared the water's edge and the trees. An electric pump was installed to pump water from the new lake to the top of the rockery, making a tumbling waterfall to feed the many pools which had been built into the scheme.

We had been propagating several hundred rock plants, and many new kinds had been bought in. When all of these were planted out in the spring even Sir Jeremiah was well pleased. Now that this part of the garden was much larger it was necessary to employ more labour, but this was no problem as most days men would come to the estate looking for work. Mr. Richards engaged three men, who were told they would be employed only for the six summer months; even so they were only too pleased to accept the job.

During the following spring Frank's health was steadily deteriorating and we were all doing our best to cover up for him. I found myself doing a lot of his work, which meant my journeymen were having to do many of my jobs. This could not go on for long, and in April a doctor was called in; he decided that Frank would have to go into hospital for tests to try to find out what was making him so tired and listless.

At first Mr. Richards was concerned about Frank's condition, but his concern turned to annoyance when he realised that Frank was going to be away for some time. He let it be known that he could not afford to have one of his key men away for any length of time, and anyway that "there was no room in his garden for invalids". His attitude shocked and surprised us, but there was nothing we could do except to say that we could manage, and to make sure Frank did not get to know what Mr. Richards had said.

Fortunately Sir Jeremiah took a more humane view of the situation when he got to know that one of his cricketers was ill, and he gave Frank six months' leave of absence. After that the job could no longer be kept open.

The situation forced our Head to make some staff changes, though they were only to be of a temporary nature. Clive took over as bothy foreman and I was appointed acting glasshouse foreman. This gave me the charge of all the flower decorating in the house, and this was an opportunity I was only too glad to accept. I was determined to take this chance to prove myself, even if I felt a little guilty at the way my chance had come.

I was now in charge of four men, and had a responsible job to hold down under the scrutiny of a clever Head Gardener. Our growing and floral work was very much in the manner of the previous year, and though there were some changes there was nothing I could not manage.

Mr. Richards gave me the opportunity to help with the staging of the display at the Chelsea Flower Show. We went up to London on the Sunday evening, and I thought we would spend the two nights we were away in a hotel. Nobody had told me the men slept in the motor-van overnight, and that we slept for only about four hours, after which we had to be back on the stand ready to help with the staging.

We did two exhibits at the Royal Horticultural Hall, so by the end of the summer I felt confident I was doing a reasonably good job and was sure I could now hold down a good foreman's position.

All this time we were taking turns in visiting Frank in hospital. It became obvious to us that he would not be returning to the bothy, and in September he was discharged, Sir Jeremiah agreeing with our Head that "the job is more important than the man". Arrangements were made for Frank to be sent home. We were sorry to lose him, but we felt he had been given a fair deal, even if it had meant Sir Jeremiah's intervention to achieve it.

I expected now to be appointed inside foreman, but I was in for a big disappointment. When I went to see Mr. Richards in his office to apply formally for the foreman's post he told me he was well pleased with my work, especially over the past six months, and he knew I was able to handle the position in question, but it was not his policy to promote anyone. He would sooner a man left and took a new appointment on another estate.

He went on to point out that if he gave me this particular job it would mean I became the bothy foreman, and I could not expect to gain the respect as foreman from my present mates that would be due to a new man. He did say, however, that when the time came he would find me a good post in another garden, so I had to be content with that promise.

Some three weeks later Rod Melling took up his appointment as our foreman. He came to us from Norman Court in Hampshire, where he had been in charge of the pleasure gardens, having gained inside experience at Lamport Hall in Northampton and at Petworth Park in Sussex. On the day of his arrival I was called into Mr. Richards' office and given to understand that he would expect me to work with, and under, the new foreman, and that he would be watching to see that I did just that.

He need not have worried, as things turned out to be much easier than might have been expected. Rod was a sensible fellow and very understanding of my position when he knew all the facts. As for myself, I saw no reason to resent him just because he had taken the position I thought I might have had, and anyway he was a bothy man, and as such we had to be friends at least. He had the good sense to allow me to do most of my growing in my own way, and he was happy to have me with him when there was decorating to do at the house. Our Head, too, could see that Rod and I had quickly come to an understanding, which developed into a firm friendship.

It was strange that Rod and I should meet in the bothy at Gatton Court, both of us having worked at Norman Court under Mr. Parsons. Having become good friends we naturally reminisced a good deal, and we agreed that we could never recommend anyone to go there to work while Mr. Parsons was the Head; for all that it was a very good garden in which to gain experience.

I gathered that Rod was a useful cricketer, but I never had the pleasure of playing with him. I still wanted to get a position as foreman and I knew I would never be happy until I achieved that objective.

I waited until Christmas was over and then went again to Mr. Richards to ask if he would help me to find such a post. He promised to do so, but told me I was not to advertise in any way as he did not want a queue of men waiting outside the garden. I asked him if he would write to some of my past Head Gardeners, but he was most indignant at this, saying that he needed no help from other Head Gardeners, he could and would place me in the right job when it came along.

Fortunately I did not have to wait very long. In the first week of April I found myself on a train bound for Worcester for an interview which resulted in my moving from Gatton Park. Mr. Richards gave me an excellent reference, saying I was well able to take a good foreman's position.

In some way I was sorry to be leaving, as the Gatton Park gardens had taught me a great deal. I had learnt much about the show business and had met many important people in the horticultural world while I was there.

# General foreman 15

SAYING farewell to my friends in the bothy, I was quite happy as I set off on my journey to the West County when I took up my appointment at Heathfield Park, some seven miles from Worcester in May, 1930. I had been engaged as general foreman by Mr. Elding, who was Head Gardener to Mrs. Scott.

The under-chauffeur met me at the station and took me to Mr. Elding's house, where Mrs. Elding invited me inside until her husband was ready to see me. My new Head was a young man, probably not much over thirty, and told me that he was in his first position as Head Gardener. He had spent fourteen years in bothy, so he knew all the little intrigues of bothy life. As his general foreman I would be bothy foreman as well as having charge of all departments under his supervision.

He talked at length about Hatfield House, Exbury, Longleat and Trent Park, which interested me more than a little. Going on to explain my duties, he told me that work started at 6.30 in the morning and went on until 5.30 from March to October; in the four winter months working time was from seven to five. I was to be paid two guineas (£2.10) a week.

No wages were paid until half past twelve on Saturday, Mr. Elding having to be satisfied that each person had worked a full week before drawing a full week's pay. The bothy would receive a coal allowance of two hundredweight each week, and this had to suffice for cooking and heating. All vegetables eaten would have to be recorded and approved by our Head, and among other things I would have to see that no lights were left on in the bothy unnecessarily.

Four men would do the garden "duties", and although I would not be expected to do any of this evening and weekend work myself I was in charge and must see that everything was done to my satisfaction, he told me. I had the power to keep a "duty" man confined to the garden if I considered this was necessary to ensure that everything was done properly.

Having had all these matters explained to me by my new Head I was sent to settle in and to meet my new workmates. The bothy was a low bungalow situated outside the kitchen garden wall and almost hidden in a small wood. It looked very dark and drab from the outside, but on entering the door I was pleasantly surprised as it was quite well furnished and decorated.

The living room was rather small, with the usual table, chairs and dresser, and the lino on the floor was almost covered with an assortment of mats which gave an appearance of comfort. This comfortable aspect was carried through into the sitting room, which boasted two sofas and three wooden armchairs. Before the open fireplace was a large brass fender with two padded leather seats at the corners which had obviously been brought to the bothy from the mansion at some time.

Having taken in the living rooms, I went into each of the three bedrooms. In each of the two larger rooms there were two beds, a chest of drawers and a cupboard for use as a wardrobe, while in the third and smaller room, which I took to be mine, there was only a single bed, with wardrobe, chest and mirror.

I was well pleased with all I had seen, and I felt I could be comfortable in this, probably the best bothy I had been in. Looking around, I felt quite sure Mr. Elding had been remembering his own bothy days when furnishing this for his men.

I gathered from what I had seen that I was to be one of five, and this proved to be so when my contemporaries came in. First to arrive was Steven Rook, who had been sent in by the Head to make sure I was settling in. A man of around thirty years of age, he was leading hand in the pleasure gardens and appeared to be a man I could rely on. After twenty minutes of near silence I began to get a feeling that while in fact I had taken the foreman's post, he felt it should have been his. I need not have worried; when I asked him if this was so, he was quick to assure me that he did not wish to have any responsibility at Heathfield Park and would be only too happy to do whatever I wished of him.

When Philip Randall, who worked with Steven in the pleasure gardens, came in I introduced myself to him. Then I met Graham Davis, leading hand in the kitchen garden, and lastly Gordon Lovelace, first journeyman in the glasshouses. Gordon was "duty" man that week, so it was he who set the table for the evening meal, at which I sat in my proper place at the head of the table for the first time. I learned a lot as we sat over that meal, and as no one seemed to want to move I was able to get a fairly clear picture of the happenings at Heathfield Park.

Our employer came in for some criticism as well as some praise, and I managed to find out something about the methods adopted by our Head in running this garden. They appeared to be much in line with what I had come to regard as normal, except for my being a "general" foreman. I got a distinct impression that this position was one of considerable importance.

Only Steven went out that evening, so by the time we retired to bed I had got to know my new mates fairly well. I could tell they were anxious to know what kind of a foreman they now had to live and work with.

One normally knew very little about one's predecessor, but the lads did tell me something of him. His name was Arthur Dunmore, and strangely enough I had followed him in at Norman Court. He had now moved on to Windsor Great Park, working in the glass-houses, but the lads were not certain what position he now held on that vast estate.

It was now my duty to take over the food bill, which varied from three to four pounds a week, and other expenditure such as cleaning materials that had been paid for by the lads. I was able to examine the grub score in detail, as my predecessor had kept all the accounts in a book. At the end of each month these accounts were shown to Mr. Elding, who then reimbursed the bothy account. I could see no good reason to carry on with this idea, so I decided to ask the bothy lady to take over these orders, then I could give the bill to Mr. Elding to settle.

A little after six o'clock the following morning I met Mr. Elding again, and he told me what was expected of me as he and I made a quick tour of the garden. There were three ranges of glasshouses, built of steel and in perfect condition. We went into two vineries, two peach houses, the fig house and on into the rose and sweet pea houses and the four plant houses, in which were growing a wide range of flowering and house plants. The tomato and chrysanthemum houses led us into the one carnation house.

All of these were lean-to structures built on walls facing east, south and west. They were not very large, the longest being no more than fifty feet, but they had a most ingenious ventilating system. Not only were there top ventilators but the whole side of each house consisted of a series of ventilators one above the other.

On the remaining side of this quadrangle was the large stone orangery housing all kinds of shrubs in pots as well as the oranges, grapefruits and lemons. In the middle of the glass ranges were five small span houses, two of them melon houses, one for cucumbers, and the others used for forcing and propagating.

This was a lot of glass for a first journeyman to have in his care. I could see I would be spending a great deal of my time in the houses, even though there were three other men and a boy to help Gordon.

The kitchen garden was much the same as the ones I had been used to. The staff of four had a garden of about two acres to manage, and as usual it was surrounded by walls. I was very pleased to know I would have sole responsibility for training and growing all the fruit trees on these walls, as the training of fruit trees is a fascinating occupation.

An avenue of Irish yews led up to the mansion, which was completely surrounded by lawns, except for the drive leading to the front door and to the tradesmen's entrance, which was at the back of the house, reached through the coal and wood yard. Beyond the lawns and in a wide circle around the mansion were different kinds of pleasure gardens, merging one into another. We passed from a rather lovely rock garden into the bulb dell, with countless spring bulbs and a great number of Liliums to give colour in the summer. This gave way to the herbaceous garden, planted in beds with three or our different kinds of plants, so that each bed had a long flowering season, and this gradually merged into a rose garden, each bed having but one variety of rose, to give a bold display.

Crossing the front drive, we went into what was known as the shrub acre. It was in this part of the grounds that I later discovered an old icehouse, built deep into a bank. On either side of the track leading to the icehouse was the dogs' cemetery, with over forty graves each with its own headstone bearing name and age, as far as was known, for it seemed several of these animals had been taken into care as strays.

The whole of this part of the garden was protected from rabbits and farm animals partly by a fence but mainly by a haw-haw, a ditch with a vertical wall on the inner side designed to be unseen from the house. It was now that I realised that this kind of protection was not so very unusual. The cattle grids set into the drives at the entrance of the garden were the first that I had seen, and I was assured that no animal would pass over them.

We finished our hurried tour in the kitchen garden and I was back in the bothy for breakfast by nine o'clock, meeting our bothy lady, Mrs. Lopas, for the first time. Steven introduced me to her, and she immediately told me she had a son who worked in the garden and proceeded to tell me what a good worker he was, no doubt hoping I would be impressed. I began to feel a little sorry for her; she was a small, rather pathetic sort of person of about fifty, who tried so hard to please. The bothy was clean and tidy, and she had prepared quite a nice meal, so I could see no reason why she should be nervous, as she undoubtedly was at our first meeting.

At first she called me "Mister"; I had to insist she called me by my christian name, as she did the rest of the lads. I asked her to sit down, as I wished to talk to her while I ate my breakfast, but she would stand, so I left it that way if she was more at ease like that. I told her that she would now do the ordering for anything she wanted in the bothy, and I would have the bills each month. I could see she was so pleased that she was now given something to do; that was very important to her, and it pleased me to know that I had given her some pleasure so early in our acquaintance.

My first job was to go to the mansion with Mr. Elding, who was to show me the floral work I was to do there. We met Mr. Pollard, the butler, who told us we were both wanted in the morning room.

It was all quite impressive, but I felt I could manage to do all that was needed, and perhaps improve on some of the designs I had seen. We went into what served as a flower room, and I felt I just had to suggest that there were some items we needed to help us do the floral work properly. I could see no sign of any canes, tying material, or wire netting, nor were there any deep buckets into which we could plunge the cut flowers. Mrs. Scott made notes of what we wanted and promised to get such things as we considered necessary.

I was to meet her every Friday morning at ten o'clock to receive orders, then in the afternoon and on Saturday morning if necessary the whole house would be redecorated ready for any weekend party that might have been arranged. It was made clear to me that I must not be in the main rooms on Saturdays after eight o'clock as guests might then be arriving, but I could work on Friday evenings if I needed to do so.

I spent the rest of that day getting to know my way around and acquainting myself with the plants that were growing in the gardens. I introduced myself to the rest of the gardeners as I came upon them. In all I found eighteen men, two boys and a lady gardener called Ruth, who was, I gathered, a widow, her husband having been killed in a farm accident.

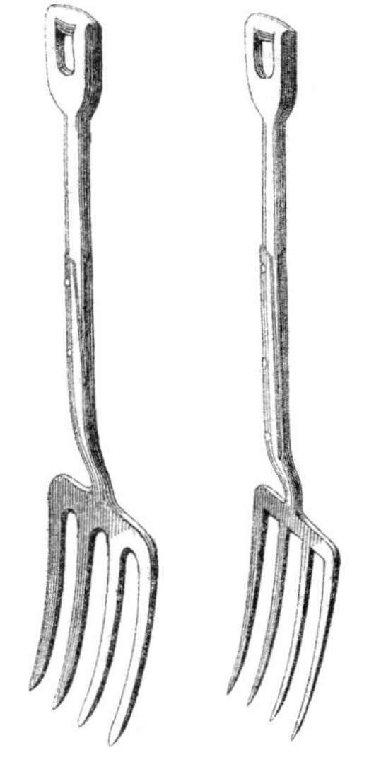

The staff here was flexible, and although there were four men and a boy in the glass-houses and a similar number in the kitchen garden, with eight more on the pleasure gardens and woodland, I was permitted to move the men and boys to any department where any special need arose. The lady gardener was, however, employed full time growing melons, cucumbers and pot plants. At first I found it a little strange to have in my charge men older than myself, but we very quickly got used to one another and no problems arose.

What I did find rather surprising was that both Mr. Scott and Mrs. Scott spent a lot of their time working in the garden. Generally they did the jobs which were pleasant to do, but on occasion they would ask Mr. Elding what needed doing, and they were quite happy doing anything, even if it meant getting quite dirty. Mr. Scott seemed to get a good deal of pleasure pushing a wheelbarrow, and whatever he or the Lady was doing they always had a barrow nearby; it seemed Mr. Scott enjoyed flexing his muscles.

I was spending very little time growing plants as the greater part of my time was taken up either with the men outside in the pleasure or kitchen gardens or in the mansion doing floral work. The Butler was very helpful, often planning his dining table to suit the flowers that were available at any given time. He would let me know in good time if there were any guests staying in the house, so that I could put flowers in their rooms before their arrival.

Mr. Pollard had on his staff two footmen and a house boy, as well as the odd-job man who attended to the boilers for central heating and domestic hot water. The housekeeper, Mrs. Brunt, had four housemaids who lived in and two daily ladies. There were four people working in the kitchen, Mrs. Topham being the Cook. Madam employed her own personal maid and Mr. Scott had his secretary, these with the two chauffeurs making up the domestic staff.

Spending as I did a lot of my time in the house I was able to see a wonderful collection of pictures, many of them portraits by important painters of years gone by. The speciality here was landscapes and seascapes by modern artists, some of them commissioned by Mr. Scott. Two small Constables were of considerable importance, as was much of the furniture, which was the work of some famous cabinetmakers. Two beautiful display cabinets were given over to a superb collection of Bristol glass. With all that to see I found much pleasure in delaying my time in the mansion whenever possible so as to enjoy all these works of art.

It was some weeks before I was able to see all of the estate, for there were many acres of woodland, with plenty of wildlife. The many species of birds were easy enough to see, they gave one time enough to look, but the animals were more difficult to find; even so one could learn a great deal about them, if only by the evidence they left behind. Fortunately no shooting or hunting was permitted on this estate, so the wildlife developed there as nature intended.

One of the two drives leading up to the mansion was known as the walnut drive as for part of the way down to the lodge gates it ran through an avenue of walnut trees. At the entrance and on both sides of the drive was a group of open plan garden cottages, eleven in all, set well back from the roadway. The lawns in front of these houses were kept in immaculate condition by the estate workers who lived there. The entrance to the station drive was similar, except that there were eight cottages and the twin lodges on either side of the gateway.

This second drive meandered through woodlands and open fields following a stream, which opened out in places into small lakes populated by an abundance of waterbirds. On the banks of the stream and the lakes wildflowers grew in profusion, and I was to learn that it was part of our job to gather wildflower seeds to sow along the sides of the stream as well as to keep under control such vigorous plants as nettles, thistles and docks which might destroy the balance of these lovely wild plants.

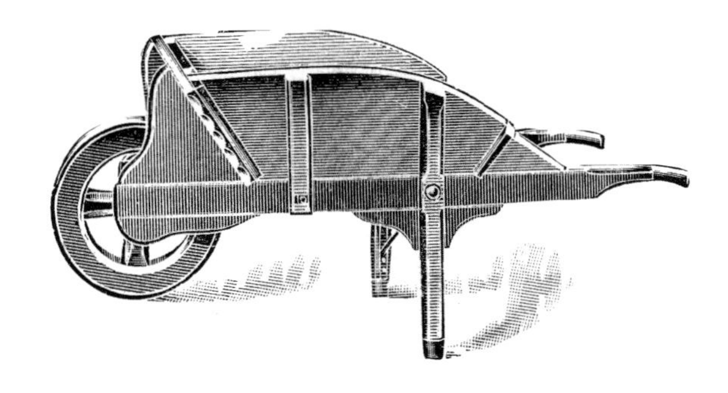

# Horses and washing up 16

THE GARAGE and stable yard near the kitchen garden were of particular interest to me, not because of the three horses that were kept for riding but because of the pleasure I derived from the team of four grey Shires that were turned out each morning in immaculate condition.

They were used mainly on the farm and in the woodlands, where timber was cut for the house fires by the woodman, who also made many hurdles, cut spars for thatching, and bundled up peasticks and bean poles. Most of these were sold, being carted away by William, the estate carter, and his team of greys, of which he was very proud.

William seldom rode in his cart but would walk for miles in front of his team carrying his long whip, which he would never use, high over his shoulder. It was a pleasure to see and hear him walking along with the four horses following with their shining brasses jingling.

William was a big strong man. It was difficult to guess his age, as he never shaved and only allowed his wife to cut his hair every second Christmas Day, or so he claimed. Not only was he the carter, he was also well known as a water diviner or dowser, and had an uncanny instinct of knowing where water should be. With his forked hazel stick held in both hands and pointing forward, he would walk around in ever-widening circles until he came to where there was water beneath the soil, at which point the hazel stick would bend downwards. This happened even when he passed over a water pipe.

One day he gave me the experience of holding one end of the stick while he held the other, and as we came to where there was water I could not stop the stick bending downwards. When left to try on my own nothing happened. William told me he did not like to do this divining too often as something seemed to drain from him when he did, and this made him very tired. All the same, whenever he was called upon to find water he would always oblige, but then he was something of a showman and liked to have an audience.

William was a genial fellow and good company, if one could put up with the strong smell of horses which prevailed all the time. When he got to know that I was keenly interested in his charges William promised me the special privilege of being around later that summer to see his baby born; William being what he was, he was referring to one of his mares and not to his wife.

We had a good summer that year, and I was reasonably happy in my new position. Perhaps because of the weather, or maybe it was something to do with our wildflower population, we had an abundance of glowworms, and it was interesting to go out at dusk and see the many hundreds of little white lights shining in the grass and along the hedgerows.

I managed to play a few games of cricket for the local village club, but my work kept me fully occupied even at weekends, with my having to make sure that all duties were done properly and that the many needs at the mansion were attended to. Most of what I did was my own work, yet I was already getting the feeling that I was doing some duties which I considered to be the Head's prerogative. On one occasion when I suggested to Mr. Elding that I might be intruding into his domain I was quickly put in my place and told to do as I was ordered. If I felt I was being leaned on, I'd better stiffen my back, he said, so I decided the best policy was to say nothing. If I was to carry some of the Head's responsibility this might serve me in good stead in the long run, when I could take on my first Head's position.

Our gardens were visited by three garden societies during the summer, and on each occasion I was detailed to show the members around for the greater part of their stay. This was something I enjoyed doing very much, as it brought me into contact with several Head Gardeners; almost invariably they were interesting people to converse with and I found the experience stimulating.

The fact that Mr. Elding put in an appearance shortly before the party left so as to accept their thanks bothered me a little, but I did not intend to let such matters worry me overmuch if I could help it, yet there came one instance when I thought I was unfairly treated. One of the men was mowing when he drove the motor mower into a lily pond, and as it was a heavy machine it was no easy matter to retrieve it. Mr. Elding was very annoyed and told me that I should give my men more attention. When I pointed out that I was in the greenhouse at the time I was told that if I could not keep my eye on the men all the time he would get someone who could, and I could clear out.

At first I felt like telling him I would do just that, but remembering the difficulty I had had in getting my job I held my tongue at that time and accepted the blame. I found this very hard to do as I felt that I should not be expected to be in two places at once. I thought that the offender should take at least some of the blame, but Mr. Elding said nothing, so it was I who had to let the man know of our Head's displeasure.

I was a little despondent for a few days, but carter William changed all that one Saturday afternoon when he came into the bothy and announced that his mare Sue was about to foal, and would I like to help him if the need arose. Making sure everything was all right in the garden and at the mansion, I hurried down to the stables. Here I found William had cleaned out a stall and was washing down with carbolic soap in very hot water. When he was satisfied everything was clean new straw was put down, but Sue was not to be allowed in there until the foal was about to be born.

We stayed with the animal all the afternoon, and late on into the evening. We had several visitors, including our employer, but William would let no one go near Sue that day. About midnight he led the mare into the prepared maternity stall, saying we would have the young one within the hour. Of course he was right, as at ten minutes to one Sue produced her infant. William did help a little during the early stages, but it was a reasonably easy birth, and the carter was a very happy man.

There was some cleaning up to do, and this done we stayed until the foal was on her feet and we had made sure Sue was all right.

Then we were able to leave mother and child to return home to get in some much-needed sleep. I spent most of that Sunday at the stables, but as everything had gone so smoothly there was nothing we really needed to do.

Monday was show day for William, and just about everyone had to see his new baby girl. Mrs. Scott came down to name the new arrival, and immediately produced a ready-painted nameplate bearing the name Victoria II, and with due ceremony wetted the filly's forehead.

During our long watch together I learned from William that it was he who was the brewmaster for the estate. Later this man of many parts took me over to his brewhouse to show me how to make beer. I knew nothing of the art of brewing, and I must confess I learned very little from him, perhaps because I was not very interested, but I did know he made a very good product as I had often had a glass of his beer when working in the mansion. He told me he made about two hundred gallons each year, and had to keep a barrel on tap in the Butler's pantry at all times, but the greater part of his brew was used on the farms at haysel and harvest time.

We managed to find another outlet for his beer when later in the year I took some men into the woods to help the woodman cut pea and bean sticks for use in our kitchen garden. It was while in these woods that we came across a large badger sett which we could see was being used by several animals, as the runs from the sett were very well used, but our wild friends kept very much out of sight.

Talking in the bothy about these badgers, Steven, Gordon and I decided to go down into the woods in the late evening to see if it was possible to get a sight of these nocturnal creatures. Although we made quite a few visits and were careful to keep downwind of the sett, the most we ever saw was the occasional fox, some hedgehogs, voles and mice, a few rats and plenty of rabbits. Some of the latter had already found their way into the bothy to help with the grub score, but after our night sojourn in the woods Gordon was keen to learn how to do a bit of poaching. I was very happy to teach him what I knew, so rabbit began to appear on our menu quite often. We were also able to get a pheasant or a duck from time to time, but we had to be very careful as we knew there would be considerable trouble should we be found out.

We had to be sure Mrs. Lopas would keep our confidence, and this we did by giving her a share of our catches. At first "Mum" was very nervous about receiving her share of the loot, but we managed to persuade her, pointing out to her that we were taking the risks and she had nothing to worry about. As to disposing of the fur and feathers, we did this when stoking the boiler late at night.

Now we thought we could catch a few dinners in reasonable safety provided we were careful, but we had reckoned without our bothy cat. He was seen in the garden eating a pheasant, and we knew it was one we had caught the previous night. We had some difficulty in convincing Mr. Elding that the cat must have caught the bird for itself, and he came into the bothy to see if there were any traces of feathers. Fortunately he found nothing, but even so it was obvious he was not entirely satisfied with our story of the cat catching the bird.

Our food bills were still too high for our liking, as we were getting little or nothing from the kitchen, so we resolved to do something about it. Once again there had to be a planned assault on the kitchen staff, as had been done many times before in most bothies. Graham was taking vegetables in to the kitchen at least once a day, so it was to be his job to soften up Mrs. Topham with flattery, at which he was very good; whenever possible he would give her a few flowers and the odd peach or two. I was able to persuade Joan, the first kitchen maid, to take an occasional walk with me when she was off duty; this I found very pleasurable, so she too had flowers and some hothouse fruit. Philip was to look after Ruby, the second kitchen maid, and they rather fell for each other and started to go steady, which suited the rest of us very well.

These efforts brought about the required dividends, and our "score" did show a marked improvement. Even so, we were not entirely satisfied with things as they were; I was not overkeen taking Joan out from time to time, and it was far from easy to get from the garden the sundry items the girls liked to have. After some discussion it was decided that the only thing to do was to get in on the washing up when we knew the kitchen staff were all very busy; it had worked before, and we could see no reason why it should not work here, and in any case these evenings spent in the "Big House" were enjoyable, up to a point, as there was usually plenty to eat and drink.

Our chance came when Mr. and Mrs. Scott gave a staff party at Christmas. All of us from the bothy were invited, but we made quite sure the Cook and her girls were spared any washing up. We rather took over the kitchen that evening, which was just as well as Mrs. Topham was pressed to drink more than was good for her and the girls were in the best of spirits and did not really want to do any work.

By that time we had really made our point, and our food bills fell even more, but the washing up did become something of a habit as time went on. Steven was the only one among us who did not take kindly to these arrangements, so we were not too sorry when in the spring he left us to take a foreman's position at Floors Castle in Scotland. We were happy for him, as we gathered that he was going to a first-class garden.

The news quickly got around that there was a vacancy in our garden, and the day before Steven moved out six men applied in person for his position. I met two of these men, one of whom had come down from Birmingham; the other had made the journey from Ascot. Mr. Elding had to put a notice on the main garden gate to the effect that no interview would be given without an appointment, yet even so not a day passed without someone trying to see the Head. It became my unpleasant duty to tell everyone who called that they were wasting their time.

Our Head seemed to be in no hurry to fill the situation, and a month passed before Bill Maitland came to us from the bothy at Norman Court in Hampshire, where I had been a few years earlier. He was a young man just twenty years old, and being used to bothy life he quickly settled down with us. We for our part were happy he had come to us as he was always so bright and cheerful, and it was not long before he relieved me by taking Joan off my hands.

Amazing as it seemed at the time, for second time someone had followed me from Norman Court. It seemed that again Mr. Parsons had more than a little to do with a man leaving his garden, but it was Bill who got himself into difficulties a little later.

For some weeks all went well, then I began to get rather disconcerted as he started to be more than just friendly with our Head's wife. Of course it was not long before people started talking about Mrs. Elding and Bill, so I thought it was time to warn him that this was not only foolish but dangerous to his future. He was not going to be put off, however; he considered life was just a game, and it was one he was going to play his own way.

We knew this situation could not last long. He had been with us for a mere three months when he was given an hour to get off the estate, and it fell to me to see that he did go within the hour. Bill didn't seem to care at all, he just packed his case and walked out, apparently still quite happy. When he had gone I had to report back to Mr. Elding that he had left the garden. Our Head never gave us any reason for packing Bill off so quickly, but I think we drew the right conclusions, as from that day on we seldom if ever saw Mrs. Elding.

We were without a lad in the pleasure gardens for another month, and once more men came into the garden hoping to get the post which was now vacant. Again the notice had to be put on the garden gate, but that did not deter some of these men. Several came into the garden, but Mr. Elding refused to see any of them, and I had to hear a few hard-luck stories. I was sure one or two of these men would have suited us very well, as they were only too anxious to show me their references, but there was nothing I could do for any of them. I did, however, learn something of the pressures that can be put on a Head when he has to engage new labour.

Later Mr. Elding told me he was going to appoint a local man who would continue to live on the estate, so from then on there were to be only four of us living in the bothy. Tom Yates came into the garden from the home farm; his recommendation must have been the superb garden he kept around his cottage near the entrance of the station drive. A man of about fifty, he soon satisfied us that he could do his work in the grounds very well, but he knew little or nothing about the weekend "duties" in the glasshouses and boiler house.

This meant I had to be with him most of the time when he came on "duty", and he was living rather far away from the mansion if things were needed in a hurry. The result of that was that it fell to me to do many of the tasks which should have been done by a "duty" man in bothy. Mr. Elding could see that Tom had difficulties in doing his "duty" week satisfactorily and promised he would alter things when an opportunity arose.

Mrs. Lopas had a second son who left school in August, and like his brother he was keen to be a gardener, so she asked me if I thought he would have a chance of being taken on and trained by Mr. Elding. I know that our Head, like any Head Gardener, would never miss a chance to get hold of a good boy, so young Ted applied to join the greenhouse staff.

Nobody was surprised when we learnt that young Ted was to be taken on, but we were all very surprised when we knew that he was to come into the bothy, though he was only fourteen. The lad was put in my care; I was not only to teach him general gardening but was to train him in bothy ways, and above all I was to see that he learned how to do the weekend and evening "duties".

I thought this was a bit much for a lad of his age, as I knew the boiler work would tax his strength to the limit, but this was an order from the Head, so Ted and I must make it work. This meant, of course, that for some months I would again have to be with the "duty man" almost all of the time, and for the most part during the early stages I would probably have to do most of the work myself.

He soon proved to be a good lad and very willing to learn, and he was always wanting to do his own work, so I was pleased to be able to help him, remembering how my own father had helped me in my early stages. I felt that here was a lad who could do well later in life, if only he had the help he needed now.

Mrs. Lopas was delighted to have her Ted with us in the bothy, and she was ever counselling him to do as he was told, but her thanking us every time her son did or learned something new was sometimes rather embarrassing.

Those of us who lived in bothies were used to changes from within, but it was not often there were changes from above, so we were somewhat surprised to be told that our Head was leaving to take up an appointment on an estate near Exeter. As a Head Gardener he was required to give one month's notice to his employer, so that gave me plenty of time to consider my position.

I decided to apply to Mrs. Scott to take over as Head. I realised I was still very young and still had very much to learn, but I felt confident I could do the job Mr. Elding was leaving, knowing that I had already carried a lot of the responsibility that should have been the Head Gardener's. Having made up my mind to try for this position I decided not to delay my application but to see an early interview. In the event the opportunity arose sooner than I had planned.

I was working in the rose garden when both Mr. and Mrs. Scott came to join me, apparently to help edge around the beds. I immediately put my request to them. They were taken by surprise and did not at first know just how to answer, then they pointed out that I was not married, and they must have a married man as Head. I assured them that I could be married in a matter of a month or two, as I was already engaged, and I was quite sure Dorothy would marry me when I could offer her a home and the assurance that I was in a good, secure job.

There the matter had to rest for the time being, as my employers felt they could not give me an answer without considerable thought, but they expressed a hope that they could rely on me to be their acting Head until they came to a decision. I hoped this was to be my chance to prove myself, and for three weeks I was left in charge.

Then one day I was called to the mansion to be interviewed by Mr. Scott, only to be told that my application would be considered along with applications from several other men. This did not sound very promising; perhaps I showed a little disappointment, because I was assured that everyone would be considered on merit. I was also told that in Mr. Elding's absence I would be expected to escort all the people who came on interview around the garden, and the appointment would be made after they had all been seen.

During the following two weeks I was introduced to five gardeners who were being interviewed. One of them was Jim Thompson, the foreman I had been under at Norman Court a few years earlier. Throughout September and most of October I remained in charge of the garden, and I knew my employers were taking note of the way the garden was being run. My hopes grew as time went on.

Then came another summons to the mansion. This time I was told by Mr. Scott that Jim Thompson had been appointed to take over as Head Gardener at Heathfield Park, without any explanation being offered as to why I had been overlooked. For the second time I had been refused a position I knew I could succeed in, having held both of them in an acting capacity.

Mr. Thompson, as I now had to address him, took over in early November and almost immediately set about making changes. For one thing he no longer wanted a general foreman. Tom was made pleasure garden foreman, Graham was given the foreman's position in the kitchen garden, and I was to have only the glass-houses in my care, helping with the floral work only when required to do so by our new Head.

He knew when he made those changes that I would not be very happy about it, but as he said, it was about time Heathfield Park gardens had a proper Head to run the gardens in a sensible manner. He realised he had put me in a difficult position by downgrading my job, and that I would find it hard to work under him for any length of time. To some extent I was an embarrassment to him, and without saying anything to me he must have started looking for a situation that would suit me.

When he told me that I was to go with him to one of the fort-nightly shows at the Royal Horticultural Hall in London I guessed he had good reason for my going. On our way up to London in the train we discussed my position with him at Heathfield Park and agreed that it was to our mutual advantage for me to move. He was quick to reassure me that I could stay with him just as long as it took for me to find the position I wanted, and that he was prepared to help me all he could. In fact we were doing the journey up to London, he told me, as he had arranged to meet two Head Gardeners who were looking for a good foreman, and it might be to my advantage to meet them.

At the show we first met a Mr. Ipson, who was looking for a pleasure ground foreman. It seemed his garden in Surrey was quite small, as he had a staff of only eight. I was not interested in going into so small a garden, and Jim Thompson also thought it would not be in my best interests to go there.

Later I was introduced to a Mr. Swan, who first wanted to know a great deal of my background. He told us something about his garden, and then invited me to go on interview to Highbury Hall, near Cambridge, where he was the Head Gardener.

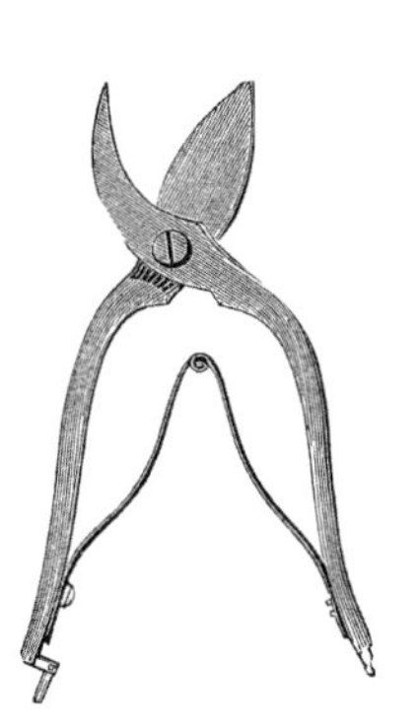

# The party season 17

THE JOURNEY by train from Worcester to London and on to Cambridge took more than six hours, so it was mid-afternoon when I arrived at the gardens of Highbury Hall in the garden motor-van, having been met at the station by one of the under-chauffeurs.

I was taken to Mr. Swan's house, and he showed me around the glasshouses and part of the pleasure garden. When it grew dark we returned to his house for, as he termed it, our little talk over a cup of tea. The interview was friendly enough, but his questions were searching, both as to my character and as to my experience. In the end I was successful in getting my second foreman's situation.

I got the job, I think, mainly because my references were satisfactory and because I had been recommended by Mr. Thompson. It did seem to help to some extent when Mr. Swan learned that I was keen to play cricket for the estate team. I was to be paid two pounds and five shillings a week, and was to do my turn on glasshouse and boiler duty, which came round every five weeks, for an extra payment of four shillings. I was to arrange the bothy "duties" to suit myself, but I must remember that it would be my responsibility to see that all "duties" were carried out to Mr. Swan's satisfaction.

I spent that night in the bothy with my new workmates, Kevin Stocks and Bert Hall, both of whom were journeymen in the glasshouses, so would be working with me most of the time. The other two occupants of the bothy were Tom Shoeman, who worked in the pleasure and rock gardens, and Eddie Rutger, who was doing his training in the kitchen garden. I was the only foreman living in the bothy, as the other three foremen were married men living in cottages on the estate.

The bothy was in a courtyard at the back of the "Big House". The five rooms were on the ground floor of what amounted to an annexe to the mansion. Above were store rooms in which, amongst many other things, was an old flint mangle which worked on the principle of pressure by weight; there was a flat bench with little drain holes and four wooden rollers supporting a large, elongated box that was full of stones. Clothes were placed on the bench and the box was pushed back and forth on the rollers to press the water out of the clothes. It was an interesting object but it could hardly have been very effective, and that presumably was why it had apparently been abandoned.

This was the first bothy I had been in which had a separate kitchen. It was quite small and had no fireplace; it looked as though most of the cooking was done on a three-burner oil stove with a portable oven covering two of the burners. When in use the stove was fed by a drop feed from an oil reservoir at one end, the fuel being supplied to the burners by gravity. The only working top in this tiny kitchen was the deep window ledge let into the thick walls, there being little room for furniture of any kind.

The three bedrooms were sparsely furnished, but at least the beds were comfortable. In the living room was an open black kitchen range which was used more for heating than cooking, perhaps because of the large crack right across the top plate and the broken oven door. A table and some chairs were the only furniture in this room, along with a row of cupboards housing all the tableware and cooking utensils. The general appearance of the place was drab. It was made to look worse because there was no covering on the floorboards, but again it was clean.

Next day I went back to Heathfield Park. I saw Mr. Thompson in the evening and was about to give him my written notice of leaving his employment when he told me there was no need for that. He was, he said, only too pleased I had accepted my new post, and added that I could go almost at once as he already had a man waiting to take my place. For my part I was glad to get away the next day so that I could spend a few days at home with my parents, and could see Dorothy once more.

This gave Dorothy and I a chance to talk over our future. Much as we would have liked to get married, we both realised that it was better I should go to Highbury Hall for a year or two, after which I could hope to get a Head's job and thus be in a good position to start our life together. My father was pleased to know I was progressing very much as he had hoped, and he too thought it wise for me to continue learning my job under a good Head Gardener for some time yet, as I was still too young to take a top job.

The following Saturday found me on my way to Cambridge, from where I was taken with my luggage in the garden van to the Highbury Hall bothy. This gave me all day Sunday to settle in and get used to my new surroundings.

Highbury Hall was a large Georgian mansion with extensive lawns and pleasure gardens. The four-acre kitchen garden also served as a nursery for growing hundreds of forest trees from seed, to up to three years old in most cases. These were in part for sale, but much of the nursery stock was planted on parts of this vast estate, where the growing and harvesting of timber was all part of a long-term plan that had been going on for many decades. The several thousand Christmas trees growing in a nearby plantation were, however, entirely for market.

The glass consisted of three ranges of lean-to houses and seven span structures, making a total of twenty-nine individual houses. I was pleased to see that five of these were given over to orchids and other exotic hothouse plants. Then there were the usual plant and fruit houses, and a great number of garden frames, most of which were heated. In one of the boiler houses was a large upright Week's tubular boiler set deep in a brick pit, with the stone stairway running down to the base of the boiler, down which the "duty" man would have to go every day to clean and clinker the fire. Fuelling was a much less arduous task, as this was done from ground level, shovelling coal down a hole on to the fire below. In the second boiler house stood two Robin Hood boilers, these also being low in the ground, but the feeding and cleaning of this type of boiler is done from the floor of the boiler house. This boiler work, with the number of glasshouses and the variety of plants being grown, would keep the "duty man" fully employed at weekends and in the evenings.

Back in the bothy I got to know my colleagues better as I talked with them about the work we were to do together. As I could see I would be kept busy most of the time I decided I would not be doing any duties in the bothy, and the boys accepted this without question. I would as a matter of course be taking charge of the grub score, which was averaging about eleven shillings a week. I made a comment about this low figure, but Eddie explained in great detail that when he took vegetables into the kitchen each morning he almost always came away with something for the bothy table. He seemed a bit nervous, almost apologetic, about this, but I was quick to assure him that I was very much in favour of this arrangement.

The boys were only too pleased to tell me about the gardens and the estate. There were thirty-three gardeners and four boys employed, and I would have five men and a boy with me in the glass department. The kitchen garden foreman, Nick Hayman, also had five men and a boy, and also had to supervise the three men working with the nursery trees; these three men also kept the drives clean and tidy. There were nine men working under Geoff Clayton in the pleasure garden, with two of the boys. Yet another foreman, Toby Corney, had charge of the rock and Japanese gardens.

I was beginning to learn quite a lot about the gardens of Highbury Hall, but our conversation was interrupted by Mr. Swan coming into the bothy. He inquired if I had settled in, but what he really wanted was for me to go with him up to the mansion to change the dining table decoration for the evening meal.

When we got there Mr. Dorman, the Butler, told us the table was ready and we could pass through the green baize door and on into the dining room. By now I was quite used to seeing superb decor in the mansions in which I had worked, but this room was by far the finest I had ever seen. There were ten beautiful pictures hanging on the walls, each with its own light above or below. The walls themselves were draped with fine pink silk of elaborate design, and the three doors carved with depictions of the three wise men were indeed a splendid sight.

The highly polished table was set for two people, with silver and cut glass, so our table centre that evening was of pink begonias, set in a silver bowl. Mr. Swan did almost all the floral work himself, but it was necessary for me to know what he needed each day from the glasshouses, and he also wished to be sure that I was able to take over the decorating should the need arise. Kevin, too, had to learn the art of flower arranging as a back-up, such was the importance of flower work in the hall.

Our work started at seven o'clock and at half past eight we went in for our breakfast. It was during that meal on Monday morning that I met our bothy lady, Mrs. Coleman, a person of about fifty whose husband worked in the kitchen garden. She was a short, rather rotund woman, and it was soon quite clear to me that we were very much "her boys", to be cared for almost as children; again it was not difficult to call her "Mum". We were to sit at table and she would place the meal before us; I gathered it was not for us to pour tea or to cut bread, that was her job, and she would spoil us if she so pleased. We appreciated it, of course, but it was hardly good training for the youngest member of the bothy, who might find things very different when he moved on.

Mrs. Coleman took it upon herself to do all our personal washing and mending, she fed the bothy cat and also found food for our tame jackdaw, the only jackdaw I had ever seen tamed. It appeared that my predecessor had reared him by hand when he was very young, and it seemed that he had adopted us rather than the other way round. He spent a lot of his time in the bothy, seemingly without fear of the cat, and was never far away. He did make a mess at times, and used to steal all kinds of small articles, but we knew his hiding place, so we were able to retrieve most of what went missing. We had to be careful not to take everything back, as we knew that if we did he would find somewhere different to hide his loot.

I had been at the hall a full three weeks before I came into contact with my employers, Mr. and Mrs. Brooks. Mrs. Brooks inquired if I was settled in for a long stay, but Mr. Brooks' only interest seemed to be his estate cricket team; he presumed I played cricket, and having got an answer in the affirmative he told me that he expected all members of the team to maintain the cricket table and the ground, outside working hours and in a rota drawn up by the Head Gardener. I was happy enough to settle for those arrangements, as it seemed quite the usual thing to do on estates where cricket was played.

It was apparent to me that here was an estate where money was spent freely on anything that was for the benefit or pleasure of our employers or their guests. Any other monies spent had to be approved by the estate agent who, it seemed to me, made sure little of this expenditure was to the benefit of the workers. In general, wages were low, and there were several cases where married men had to manage on twenty-eight shillings a week. Most of the cottages were in need of repairs, and some were even in a dilapidated state; in some cases a nearby water tap was something of a luxury, so it was little wonder that our bothy was poorly furnished and rather drab. There was little Mr. Swan could do about it if the estate agent refused to spend the money.

This did not bother us all that much, as we who lived in bothies did not expect too much comfort. We were there to learn our profession, and this was a superb garden for gaining experience. I was spending a lot of my time in the orchid and fruit houses, and our Head was ever ready to give me the benefit of his superb knowledge. My growing programme fascinated me to such an extent that at times I had to be reminded that I was needed in some other part of the garden, at the hall, or on occasion even on the cricket field.

I managed to get in a few games during May and early June, but we were not a very good side. Only three or four of us played to win, so we lost most times, and my interest did flag somewhat. Then for five weekends from the middle of June Mr. and Mrs. Brooks gave garden parties to their country friends, which meant that Mr. Swan and his four foremen never had an hour off duty during the party season.

Usually about a hundred people were invited to these elaborate affairs, and for the first time I came to realise that the parking of motor-cars could be a problem. We had to make sure the whole garden and the glasshouses were immaculate.

The garden near the Hall and all the glasshouses were lit up with fairy lights, and the large summerhouse was converted into a bar, the buffet being in the front hall of the mansion. If the weather was good dancing on the lawn to a six-piece band seemed to be favoured by most of the guests, but the beautiful panelled ballroom was always made ready for use in case the weather forced the dancers indoors.

Although we had to be on hand, as workers we were not to be seen, except early on Sunday morning when we had to clear any debris left behind in the garden or the greenhouses. In a way we enjoyed these parties, as some of the luxuries from the buffet and bar somehow found their way into our bothy, and we were a little proud to show off our efforts in the garden to so many important people. Our collection of exotic plants and our little weather station were points of interest to many of the guests.

This was my second garden which made returns of weather conditions to the Meteorological Office, and I now realised that there was quite a number of estates throughout the country which did this work in an unofficial capacity.

During the summer I had a new interest almost thrust upon me. Mr. Swan decided he would go in for beekeeping, and he asked me if I had enough interest to help him from time to time. I soon fell under the spell of these marvellous insects and became eager to learn all I could about them.

Mr. Swan was no expert, so we joined the local beekeepers' association and got lots of advice from them. We got to know enough about bees to be reasonably successful, but even so we had to learn from experience, rather bitter experience in one case. We had two of our hives down in the orchard that first year, and both seemed to be doing well in June, honey was flowing in both, so we left them alone until July. Mr. Swan decided then that it was time to take some of the honey, but when we opened the orchard hives we found to our amazement and dismay that one of them was completely empty, yet some bees were still working.

We called in an expert who seemed to know at once exactly what was happening. There must be a strong wasps' nest nearby, he said.

We looked around and, sure enough, we found two within thirty yards of our hives.

He told us how bees would fight to keep other insects out of their home, but once wasps had made an entrance into the hive and had got the smell of the hive on to their bodies the bees would allow the wasps to take their honey without protest. This proved to be perfectly correct, since when we destroyed the wasps with cyanide our bees began to store honey again.

That honey, of course, we had to leave for their own winter feed. Our other hives, which had not been robbed, gave us more than thirty pounds of good honey, which we considered to be highly satisfactory for our first year.

It took me many weeks to discover even half of this vast estate, most of which was surrounded by a wall said to be some five miles long. There was a great variety of wildlife in the woods, on the open pasture and on the lake and ponds, and as no gamekeepers were employed the birds and animals and their predators lived to establish their own balance. Pheasants, snipe, partridge and woodcock bred naturally on the estate, while waterfowl occupied the lake and the various lesser ponds.

There were more than fifty cottages for estate and farm workers, the one large farm being managed by Mr. Sekin. He had two farm bailiffs, one of them concerned with the many acres of arable land, almost all of which lay outside the long wall. A Mr. Tyler was bailiff inside the wall, where there was pasture land for horses and many cows; this was a dairy enterprise, with women employed in the dairy to make butter, cheese and whey. Milking was done by machine, but it was no longer done by portable machines in the field. Milking parlours had been established as part of the dairy, and the animals presented themselves at milking time, then went to their respective places in the parlour, where they were fed while being milked. The milk was piped from the cow into a glass-lined tank in which it was cooled and stored before being put into churns for rail transport to London.

When grouse shooting started Mr. and Mrs. Brooks went to Scotland for six weeks, not so much for the shooting as for a holiday; they were not great sportspeople. That was also our holiday time; we were each given one week paid holiday. Just as had happened before, two of the bothy lads did not know what they were going to do with a whole week off, but they both settled to stay in the bothy and spend the days cycling around the local countryside.

I went back home for my week. During all that week Dorothy and I could talk of little except the time to come when we could marry. We tried to make plans of what we would do when that time came, but we could make little progress since we had no idea where we would be when that time did arrive.

Dorothy seemed happy to leave it to me to decide when we could start life together, and she was quite prepared to set up home wherever I could find a suitable post. This gave me even more incentive to try for a Head's position before too long, but we agreed that if this could not be obtained we would settle for a married foreman's position.

I said I thought I would need at least another year's experience, so I went back determined to learn all I could in the time I had left in bothy.

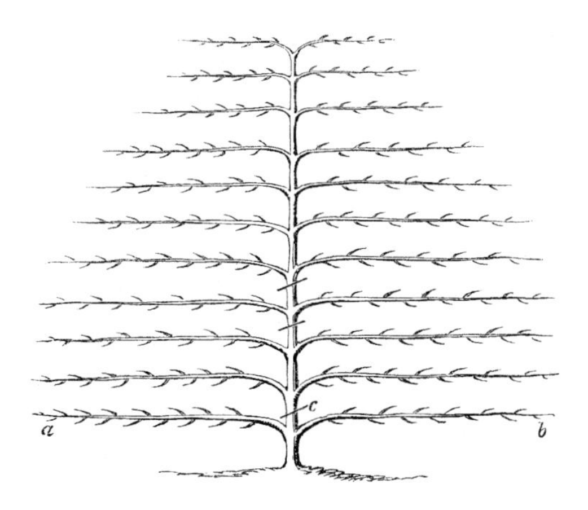

# Leaving the bothy 18

I WORKED hard that winter, hoping to make a good impression on Mr. Swan, on whom I would have to rely to some extent to help me get a good position. I knew he was the kind of person who would help if he was sure the job offered was right, and I had proved to be worth his confidence. He demonstrated this later when he found Kevin his first foreman's job at Arundel Castle.

Kevin's place in the bothy was taken by Allen Maykin, who came from Petworth House in Sussex. Bert Hall was now made first journeyman under me, and Allen took over as second. He had been well trained at Petworth, so he fitted in very well and was able to do his 'duty' turns without too much supervision.

We had a severe winter that year, so our boilers were hard pressed to keep the inside temperature up to the mark. It was our putting this extra load on the boilers that caused one of our Robin Hoods to break down. We were able to shut that one off, but the second one was not big enough to hold the heat in the orchid and store house, and we would have been in considerable trouble had it not been for our oil stove from the bothy, supplemented by various oil lamps we managed to find in the mansion.

I expected we would have to carry on using these emergency lamps for some time, so I was very concerned for "Mum" trying to do the cooking on the old cracked kitchen range. Our difficulties were quickly conveyed to our employer, who lost no time in taking action. One telephone call from him to a firm in Cambridge and they were there in two days to replace the broken section, even though they had had to go up to Birmingham to get the new part.

The cold weather did have its recompense, as we were able to go skating on the lake, though not before one of the farm bailiffs had proved the ice to be safe. This he did by drilling to find the thickness of the ice; when he had drilled almost to the underlying water there was a loud crack-then he was satisfied that people could skate safely on the ice. The lake was a great attraction for people from many miles away for quite a few days, but in the end Mr. Brooks had to order a curfew at half past eleven as some people wanted to stay on the ice all night. Of course we were sorry when the thaw did come, but at least we could now have some peace when darkness fell.

The winter gave way to spring very reluctantly, and on the nights of 13th and 14th May we had some very hard frosts that did considerable damage to some of the fruit and vegetable crops. Everyone was called out to cover up all the tender plants with straw and anything else we could find, and we did manage to save the strawberry crop and some of the other fruits, but a great deal had to be written off. The kitchen garden staff were forced to set about replanting many of their crops.

One evening a man came storming into the bothy and demanded to see Bert Hall. I had to remind him that he could not just walk into our bothy, and told him that if he had anything to say I would hear him outside. Eventually, after quite a verbal tussle, he was persuaded to go back to the door, and then I asked him his business.

He said he wanted to see Bert Hall about his daughter, and when I told him that Bert was not in he said he would wait until he came in. Our visitor was beginning to calm down, so I invited him inside and suggested he tell me what the trouble was. Without more ado he told me that Bert had been "messing about" with his daughter, and he intended to see that Bert married the girl.

At that I inquired if she was in "a certain condition", to which he said "she'd better not be!" I pressed the question, and gathered that the father did not think his daughter was pregnant, which made me wonder what all the excitement was about.

Bert came in about an hour later, by which time our visitor was more in control of himself, but even so the exchanges between the two men were quite heated. I did not want to interfere in the argument but I had to be on hand; whatever happened in the bothy was my responsibility, and the last thing I wanted was an exchange of blows between the two men. By then all the lads had retired to their rooms, but I knew that everyone was listening and ready to come to Bert's assistance if necessary; such was the bothy code.

It was some time before the girl's father left and I was able to ask Bert the outcome of the encounter. He told me that they had settled their differences by Bert agreeing not to see the girl again, but it had upset the lads to have witnessed this row inside the bothy.

A few days later it was our "'Mum" who was in tears. Her husband had said she was to give up her job in the bothy and to spend more time at home, so she now had to give me notice of her leaving. I told her that if she had to resign she must give her notice to Mr. Swan, as he was her employer, but she said she could not face our Head and implored me to do it for her. So for her sake I took it on myself to tell Mr. Swan, who was most displeased at this news. He said he would see the woman's husband at once, and the man was called into the office.

It seemed that a good deal of pressure was put on him to allow his wife to continue in her job, and as usual he had to give way to authority, so "Mum" stayed with us. It was a wonder she did stay, because about a couple of weeks later she had the shock of her life.

She came running into the garden screaming something about a cat. The first person she found was Bert, who at first could not make out what was wrong, so he ran back to the bothy with her. He found the oven door open and our bothy cat dead inside.

It appeared that the cat must have crept into the oven some time the previous evening or during the night, when it was still a little warm. At some time, we could not be sure when, someone must have shut the oven door; we could never be sure who it was, though each of us searched his memory to try to work out who the unlucky person could have been who closed that fatal door. In the morning the fire was lit as usual and enough coal put on to last an hour or so, and we all went off to work, unwittingly leaving our poor cat to roast. We would have liked to have thought she suffocated in the oven overnight, but with the cracked oven door this could not have been so and we just had to face up to the agony that poor animal had suffered.

Everyone on the estate was horrified to hear of such a terrible thing, but for us in the bothy it was beyond belief. That was the only time I ever saw men ill at the death of an animal, and without really knowing it I think we all wanted to get away from that bothy.

It was fortunate that the busy season was with us and we could immerse ourselves in our work. The Chelsea Flower Show was a great place for some of us to forget our troubles, and Mr. Swan took Bert, Eddie and me to spend a wonderful day at this, the greatest spring show in the world. This time I discovered that one of the beer tents, the Ranelagh Bar, was a meeting place for gardeners, and here I was introduced to several Head Gardeners; I also met up with their foremen. It gave us all a great deal of pleasure to compare notes about the gardens we were working in and the Head Gardeners under whom we were working, or had worked. Information of this kind was vital to all of us who were living in bothies and training to become Heads.

Here was the place to find the representatives of all the big seed and sundries firms. I met up with four of these men over a glass of beer, so I was able to sound them out about any Head Gardeners' situations that might be likely to fall vacant. All four told me that there were too many good gardeners chasing after very few jobs, but each of them promised he would not forget me as he travelled about. They were all men who knew all that was going on in gardens throughout the country, so I was ever hopeful that something would in due course come of our meeting.

The time not having yet come when I felt I could ask Mr. Swan to help me in my quest, I continued to try to give satisfaction that summer. In many respects it was a repeat of the previous year. Eddie left us in August for a foreman's position on an estate near Perth in Scotland, and his place was taken by Ronald Mooney, who joined us from Burghley House, near Stamford.

Ron was a very good cricketer, more than just useful with the bat, and he considerably strengthened the estate side for the rest of that season. He told us that, judging from his interview, his ability to play cricket was a major point in his favour and had resulted in his getting the job. It seemed that someone in authority was getting a bit concerned at our lack of success on the field. The team was further strengthened by the inclusion of a new farm hand, who took over behind the stumps; he was also capable of making some useful runs when it came to our turn to bat.

By late September I was restless once more, so I wrote to the leading seed firms to inquire if they had any suitable vacancies on their books. Their replies were not encouraging, and I was rather forced to ask Mr. Swan for help. He was not very happy at the thought of my leaving, and made it clear he thought I should stay with him for another year or two. I began to wonder if in fact I had made myself too useful, though he did say he would not stand in my way.

I answered all the advertisements in *The Gardener's Chronicle* that looked promising, but to little avail. My lack of success caused me to resign myself to spending another Christmas at Highbury, but then in the New Year I got a letter from one of the seed firms advising me to apply for a Head's position in a garden near Godstone, in Surrey. I wrote off, sending copies of all my references.

To my delight I got a letter asking me to go on interview. I told Mr. Swan, and he gave me a provisional reference to take with me when I went to Godstone two days later for an interview with Mr. Petting, who showed me around his small garden. It was a neat and tidy little garden with but six glasshouses, and employed only five men. I was sure I could manage the garden and expressed a wish to accept the post, but Mr. Petting was not to be hurried.

It seemed that I was only one of seventeen men who had applied, and he intended to pick his man in his own time. He told me that he would write and let me know his decision later. When his letter did arrive it informed me that Mr. Petting considered me to be too young to be a Head and he was turning down my application.

As it seemed to be my age that was the trouble, I put on three years when applying for situations. I did get two more interviews, but in spite of my advancing my age each of the appointments went to an older man.

Dorothy and I were very disappointed, so we decided that I had better get a post as a married foreman for two or even three years.

When I told him of our decision Mr. Swan agreed it would be to my advantage to take a married foreman's situation until I was much nearer thirty years of age, when my chances of a Head's post would be so much better.

He strongly advised me not to accept a position as Head in a small garden such as I had seen at Godstone, but to wait and gain more experience. Have a little more patience, he told me, then he was sure he could find me a good foreman's job, provided I was prepared to go anywhere. This made good sense to me, and I was happy to agree.

With the start of another cricket season we were a much better side. Tom Shoeman had left us for another journeyman's position at Belvoir Castle in Leicestershire, and the new man, Simon Leach, proved to be a cricketer of some ability. He was already twenty-one but had had only three years' garden experience at Harewood House, in West Yorkshire, and felt that he had lost three good years working in a factory. It seemed that in his case, too, it was his cricket that had helped a good man obtain a position with us, and he was keen to do well in his first job living in a bothy.

Chelsea Flower Show came once more. This time it was to change the pattern of my life. Before we separated to have a look around the show I was told to be sure to meet Mr. Swan in the beer tent at three o'clock, and when I arrived I found him in conversation with a Mr. Foot, to whom I was introduced. He was Head Gardener to Mr. Chettle, a tea merchant, at Alderbrook Park, near Cranleigh, in Surrey.

Mr. Foot seemed to be interested in my career so far, and after some discussion he invited me to go to Cranleigh for an interview in his own garden. I had to wait a whole month before I could go to Cranleigh, and that gave me time to tell Dorothy and my parents what was happening.

When the day came I got a fast train from Cambridge to London, took the underground to Charing Cross and a Southern Railway train to Guildford, where I arrived soon after midday. I had been told to look for a red van, so I went in search of it and, finding it outside the station, was taken to Alderbrook Park. This was another big estate, with a large garden employing twenty-nine men and boys. All the glasshouses were span type, which meant fruit trees covered all the walls around the three-acre kitchen garden.

After a long interview I was offered the position of hardy fruit and kitchen garden foreman, with a staff of four men and a boy. My wages were to be two pounds ten shillings (£2.50) a week, and I was to have a free house and free vegetables; I was also to be supplied with one ton of coal a year and twenty gallons of paraffin.

I was told that I had to take up the post within five weeks, and in that time I had to be married and to occupy the house provided. This was a large three-bedroom house, with sitting room, kitchen and scullery. The cooking range and a free-standing bath were in the scullery; the sink and dresser were in the kitchen, which would also serve as the dining room. The house stood on its own about a quarter of a mile from the mansion, with its own ample garden. Looking at it, I could see we would have no neighbours.

I was able to assure Mr. Foot that we could take possession and move in within the time allowed, so the job was mine. I returned to Cambridge that same day, and having got there I had to set about making the necessary arrangements to get married. I was able to give Dorothy a detailed description of the house we would have at Alderbrook Park, but I could see no way in which my future wife would be able to see the house for herself before we moved in.

I lodged on the estate for the four weeks up to the wedding to get the banns read in the church and to furnish the house. At a cost of £100 I bought furniture for the two bedrooms, the sitting room and the kitchen/dining room, plus pots and pans and enough food to last a few days.

Then, on Friday the 9th of February, 1934, I went to Salisbury and stayed the night with my parents. Dorothy and I were married in St. Thomas's Church, Salisbury, at midday the next day, and we had our reception in the afternoon, then had to catch a train at 5.30 for Guildford. As I was required to start work two days later there was no chance of us having a honeymoon, so we employed what was left of the weekend settling into our home.

As I said, it was a fairly secluded house, and Cranleigh was nearly three miles away, a long walk there and back. We had no transport, so it was as well I had got in enough food for us to live on as the thought of that long walk back with a full shopping bag put us off the idea of shopping. Not that we really needed to go shopping in town, since in those days most of our food, and many of our other needs, was brought to the door.

We were not in that house very long, but it has happy memories for me, because it was there that our son was born in May, 1935.

* * *

So the time had come for me to leave the bothy for good. I had enjoyed nearly eleven years in bothy, and in many ways I was sorry to leave the life that I had grown used to. I had had to work hard and at times to put in many unpaid hours; sometimes things had not been too comfortable; yet I had been given the opportunity to work under some excellent Head Gardeners who had taught me all about the one job I love doing. I knew I would miss the comradeship of all the men I had known, worked with and lived with in the bothy, but the time had come for me to start a new life.

# Head Gardener at last 19

AFTER only two years at Alderbrook Park I moved to Ford Manor at Lingfield, a few miles north of East Grinstead in Surrey, as deputy Head Gardener under Mr. Gooding, who was Head Gardener to Colonel and Mrs. Clay. The big garden at Ford Manor, famous for its rhododendron and shrub garden, in which every path was covered with moss, employed twelve men and two boys. We also had quite a collection of new and untried daffodils.

Mrs. Clay was a member of the Astor family and Colonel Clay was MP for Tunbridge Wells, so it was natural that politicians and other famous people were among those invited to parties in the mansion.

I spent nearly three years at Ford Manor, at the end of which I had reached the magic age of thirty and began looking for my first Head Gardener's position. I found it not too far away, at Hookstile House, Godstone, the home of a Mr. Horler, with a staff of three.

My stay there was short lived, however, because of the outbreak of the Second World War in the autumn of 1939. Mrs. Horler collected her three children and went off to their other estate in Devon, and within a few days Mr. Horler decided to join his wife. As a result of this he closed down our estate, giving everybody one week's notice to leave the garden and the houses we were living in.

That put Dorothy and me, and others, in something of a predicament. I informed my father, who by that time had taken over the several gardens at the Old Manor, a rather large mental and psychiatric hospital at Salisbury, of our situation, and in reply he asked me if we would go to Salisbury to help him. He had already lost four of his men who had been called up for the Forces, and he could do with my help, at least until I too was called up. I was happy to do so, particularly as Dorothy and our little son would be near her family and mine.

So it was that I took over as foreman in the Old Manor's four-acre vegetable garden, looking after patients who were working in the gardens as part of their therapy. Of course the gardening was not merely part of their treatment, it was producing food for the 250 other patients in the hospital. As I said, I had taken on the job until I was called up, but once I was in the job I discovered that as a producer of food I was in a reserved occupation. Not only was I not to be called to the Forces, I would not be able to move jobs until the war was over.

In southern England we soon found ourselves in the front line. Though I was in a reserved occupation I could join Civil Defence, and I went into the First Aid and Rescue Squad, so I was on call 24 hours of every day.

When I got my release I resumed my search for a Head's job, and was able to find a Head Gardener's situation in Hertfordshire, going to take over the garden at Green End House, near Ware, for Mr. Hanbury. Things had changed since my days in bothy when a large garden employed twenty or thirty men or more, and many gardens had suffered severely during the war. I had a staff of only four, but the garden had been well kept, it still had good glass-houses, and the cottages were in good order.

Mr. Hanbury said he would like to show at the Royal Horticultural Society, and asked me if I thought we could do so. This was just the thing I was looking for, so once again Green End was represented at the RHS shows, at which I was able to win two Hogg Medals for Mr. Hanbury.

I was very happy with Mr. Hanbury, but I still hankered after something bigger. This I found in 1950 at Tyntesfield, near Bristol, as Head Gardener to Lady Wraxall. These very important gardens employed a staff of ten, and there I was able to grow many different species of plants, most of which were needed for the many garden parties in summer and the indoor parties during the winter. I had quite a lot of super glasshouses for fruit and some vegetables, as well as the vast number of bedding plants needed for the pleasure garden.

I stayed with Lady Wraxall for nearly six years, and then I had the opportunity to take over the gardens of the RHS president, Sir

David Bowes-Lyon, at St Paul's Waldenbury, back in Hertfordshire, not far from where the new town of Stevenage was growing up. This, of course, was an opportunity not to be missed and gave me a big lift in the horticultural world.

Those gardens were well known and much visited by important people, including royalty. Good as my job was, it was somewhat stressful at times and two years was as long as I wanted to stay. I had little difficulty in finding another post, so we moved to Fanshaws, near Hertford, for Mr. G. Barclay, the banker. It was not such a big garden as the one at St Paul's Walden Bury, but it employed six men and was well kept and well funded. Again it was a garden of much interest.

I had been with Mr. Barclay less than two years when he died. The estate and garden were taken over by the Institute of the Motor Industry, but happily for me this did not mean a change of staff, and they proved to be good employers. The situation suited me, and I stayed there until I retired in 1975.

**Fanshaws, near Hertford, where I remained until my retirement.**